W9-CMP-026

The Book of
Paper
Quilling

The Book of
Paper
Quilling

Techniques &
Projects for Paper Filigree

Malinda Johnston

Sterling Publishing Co., Inc.   New York
A STERLING/LARK BOOK

Editor: Chris Rich
Art Director: Kathleen Holmes
Production: Elaine Thompson, Kathleen Holmes, Charlie Covington
Illustrations: Malinda Johnson and Charlie Covington
Photography: Evan Bracken, Light Reflections, Hendersonville, NC

Library of Congress Cataloging-in-Publication Data
Johnston, Malinda.
     The book of paper quilling : techniques & projects for paper
filigree / Malinda Johnston.
          p.   cm.
     "A Sterling/Lark book."
     Includes indexes.
     ISBN 0-8069-0598-0
     1. Paper quillwork.   I. Title
TT870.J64   1993
745.54--dc20   93-37240
                                                    CIP

10 9 8 7

A Sterling/Lark Book

First paperback edition published in 1995 by
Sterling Publishing Company, Inc.
387 Park Avenue South, New York, N.Y. 10016

Produced by Altamont Press, Inc.
67 Broadway Asheville, NC 28801 (828) 236-9730

© 1994 by Altamont Press

Distributed in Canada by Sterling Publishing
     % Canadian Manda Group, One Atlantic Avenue, Suite 105
     Toronto, Ontario, Canada M6K 3E7
Distributed in Great Britain and Europe by Cassell PLC
     Villiers House, 41/47 Strand, London WC2N 5JE, England
Distributed in Australia by Capricorn Link (Australia) Pty, Ltd.
     P.O. Box 704, Windsor, NSW 2756 Australia

Every effort has been made to ensure that all the information in this book is
accurate. However, due to differing conditions, tools, and individual skills,
the publisher cannot be responsible for any injuries, losses, and other
damages which may result from the use of the information in this book.

Printed in China
All rights reserved

Sterling ISBN 0-8069-0598-0 Trade
                 0-8069-0599-9 Paper

Table of Contents

Introduction

Quilling (also known as paper filigree) was born over five hundred years ago, when artists discovered that narrow strips of paper could be rolled, scrolled, fluted, and fringed, and then arranged on their edges to create beautiful designs. Since that time, thousands of people, including nuns, housewives, and at least one English princess, have discovered the rewards of paper filigree. Today, though quilling tastes, tools, and even materials have changed, this fascinating art form still thrives.

Unlike the quillers of centuries past, contemporary quillers no longer face the inconvenience of having to hand-cut their paper strips. Paper is now machine-cut and sold in a splendid array of colors. Modern tools have made rolling and fringing much simpler, too, and for hobbyists who don't have time to create original designs, craft shops and quilling suppliers carry patterns to suit every possible taste. What's more, quilling is inexpensive; many of the tools and materials that you'll need are everyday household items.

Perhaps quilling's greatest attraction, however, is that it's just plain fun. With a little patience, a few pieces of colored paper, and this book, you'll soon discover that this craft is as easy to learn and as close to fail-safe as a craft can get. A quilling mistake never costs more than a few minutes' time to repair, and a quilling success is almost incredibly versatile: it can hang on a wall, decorate a box, embellish a gift card, be suspended from a window or doorway, or even deck a holiday wreath.

Within these pages, you'll find a thorough introduction to tools, materials, and techniques. Once you've learned the basics of shaping paper, a practice session will prepare you for the exciting projects that follow. Ranging from photograph borders and refrigerator magnets to earrings and Christmas tree decorations, these projects come complete with patterns, clear step-by-step instructions, and color photographs. If you'd like to try your hand at creating original designs, the "Gallery" chapter, which includes some of today's best quillwork, will offer all the inspiration you need. In less time than you might think, you'll be joining the hundreds of men and women who now count quilling as their favorite pastime.

History

Too often, the crafts of yesteryear fade away. Tastes change with time, interest dwindles, and skills are lost. Quilling, however, is one of the fortunate few that have survived. Although paper filigree has seen its periods of decline, and although very little early quillwork has been preserved, this age-old craft continues to provide immense pleasure to the people who now practice it.

The act of quilling paper is fairly simple. Strips of paper are first rolled around a needle-like instrument. Years ago, feather quills were probably used for this purpose. The rolls are then shaped, turned on edge, and arranged on a background of fabric, paper, or wood. When did paper filigree first appear? Because little of its history has been recorded, we can't be sure. Most of the quillwork now in museums dates from the eighteenth or nineteenth century, yet evidence suggests that quilling has existed for at least five hundred years.

The ornate rolls and scrolls of quillwork were most likely inspired by metal filigree, the art of shaping fine silver and gold wires into delicate, open designs. Handmade papers were far less costly than these precious metals but could be shaped in similar ways. Quilling therefore proved to be an aesthetically pleasing and economical alternative to the elaborate metal art it resembled. To emphasize this resemblance, some quillwork was even gilded.

The first quillers were probably members of European religious orders. These cloistered nuns and monks created art of a religious nature and therefore had access to precious materials set aside expressly for this purpose, materials that were much less readily available within the secular world. And among these materials were handmade papers, less precious than gold or silver, certainly, but far more valuable than machine-made papers are today. Reliquaries

Shield-Shaped Picture, Circa 1790
20 x 16 inches (50.8 x 40.6 cm)
Courtesy Florian Papp Gallery, New York

The shield shape sometimes served as a fire screen. Marks on this shield's back indicate that it was probably fitted with a pole and clamp that allowed it to be adjusted by the person who wished to be screened from a fire. The floral composition, a still life surrounded by a vine, rests on a white silk ground. A three-dimensional effect is created by the layered shapes and by the angled spiral rolls. The twisting of paper around the vine stem is one of several variations that make this piece artistically unique.

Oval Cribbage Board, Late Eighteenth Century

1-1/4 x 5-1/4 x 7-3/4 inches (3.2 x 13.3 x 19.7 cm)
Courtesy Florian Papp Gallery, New York

During the eighteenth and nineteenth centuries, cribbage was a popular card game, one in which the game's progress was recorded by inserting pegs in a board. This boxwood board, with its delicate "rope" string inlay, surrounds an oval filigree floral panel on a crushed, white glass background. The counting pegs were stored in a hidden compartment on the board's underside.

Small Mahogany Cabinet, Circa 1800-1810

13-1/2 x 9 x 14-1/4 inches (34.3 x 22.9 x 36.2 cm)
Courtesy Florian Papp Gallery, New York

Custom cabinetmakers sometimes constructed furniture with recessed panels so that the owner could incorporate filigree decoration. The doors of this cabinet open to display graduated, ivory-handled drawers, each with a 3/8"-deep front to accommodate 1/4" rolled paper coils. The excellent condition of the quillwork can probably be attributed to the protection offered by the doors.

embellished with intricate paper scrollwork can still be found in European museums.

By the late eighteenth and early nineteenth centuries, paper was more widespread and much less costly. Its use in decorative crafts burgeoned, especially in England. There, quilling was considered to be an appropriate hobby for the fashionable ladies of the time. As a result, many women of the upper and middle classes became expert quillers. At least one women's magazine described paper filigree in some detail, and others published patterns. Princess Elizabeth herself gifted her physician with a quilled screen, one which is now at the Victoria & Albert Museum. And even novelist Jane Austen, in *Sense and Sensibility* (1811), refers to a "fillagree" basket.

As well as baskets, other everyday items were elaborately decorated with quillwork: tea caddies of various shapes and sizes, trays, fire screens, and furniture. One tea caddy, in a collection of eight at the Victoria & Albert Museum, is kept in its original box. The papers' vivid colors have therefore been preserved and offer fine testimony to the skill and creativity of the caddy's maker.

Paper filigree pictures were also popular; coats of arms and floral designs were favorite themes. Many designs combined quilling with other paper-craft items: cut-paper flowers, folded paper, crimped paper (pressed into small ridges), and huskings (loops made by wrapping paper around upright pins). Furniture, too, was decorated with quillwork, which was set into recessed areas in cabinet doors and drawers.

Quilling spread from England to the American colonies, where it found a home in the New England area. So popular did this craft become that newspaper advertisements for some boarding schools listed "Quill-Work" among

Lady's Purse or Work Basket, Circa 1789
9 x 4 x 10 inches (22.9 x 10.2 x 25.4 cm)
Courtesy Florian Papp Gallery, New York
This charming creation may have been used to hold sewing threads and bits of fabric or lace, or possibly as a handbag. One side of the boat-shaped base is covered with quilled pink and red flowers and green leaves. The date (1789) has been worked into the design. On the opposite side is an embroidered floral pattern.

Rectangular, Cut-Corner Tea Caddy, Circa 1790
6 x 5 x 7-3/4 inches (15.2 x 12.7 x 19.7 cm)
Courtesy Florian Papp Gallery, New York
Judging from the large number that survive, tea caddies appear to have been popular bases for quillwork. Small medallions were often incorporated in the best of these; this example displays a colored mezzotint of a drummer boy. Though published quillwork patterns existed at the time, many of the caddies still extant include distinctive and original variations.

the subjects taught. Most of the American pieces still in existence are sconces (wall brackets for candles) that were made during the period between 1825 and 1850. The quillwork on these was often embellished with shells, wax flowers, twisted wire, and mica or ground glass. The fine particles of rock and glass must have looked wonderful by candlelight.

In the Colonial Williamsburg collection, in Williamsburg, Virginia, there are two cribbage boards, made sometime between 1790-1810, a late eighteenth century tea caddy, and an English three-dimensional picture of a castle. A document discovered inside the castle states: "To the person who destroys this paper-fillagree castle built at Nottingham. This castle built in the year of our Lord 1789 by Susanna the wife of Will III Streetton during the imprisonment of the Royal Family of France in the Thuilleries, and in the memorable year in which the Bastile was destroyed."

For reasons that aren't clear, quilling's popularity seems to have faded during the late 1800s. Not until the middle of this century did quilling re-emerge. Today, thanks to the enthusiasm, knowledge, and skills of quillers everywhere and to the Quilling Guild of England (including members from around the world), this captivating craft is back to stay.

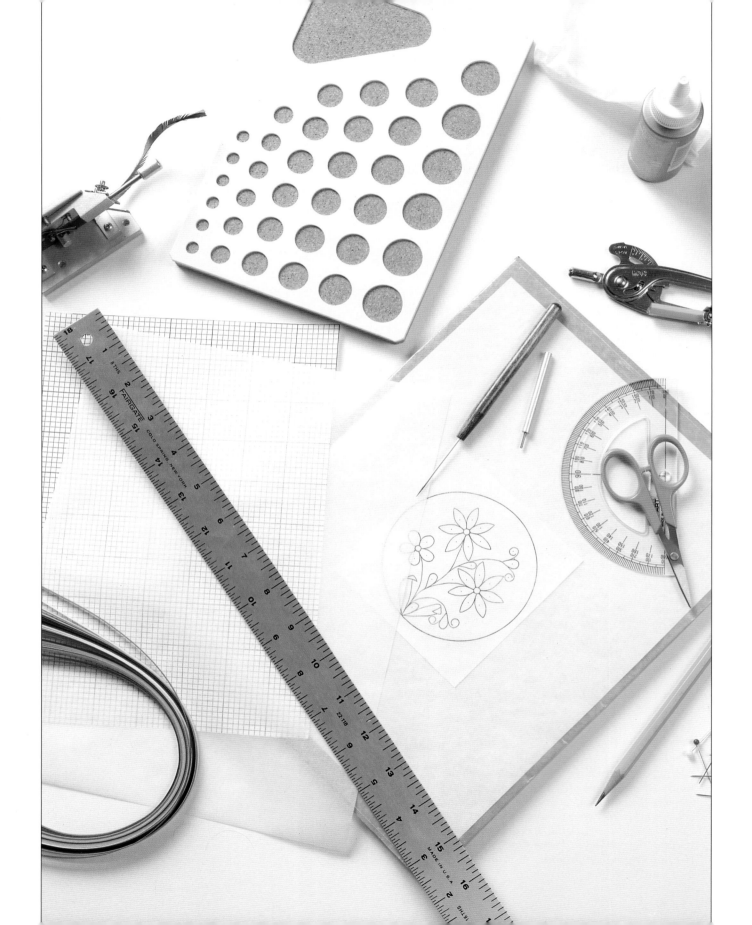

Getting Started

The basics of quilling are just that—basic. They don't take years to learn. What does quilling take? Surprisingly little. In fact, two functional hands, some colorful strips of paper, one quilling tool, and a few supplies will get you off to a great start. Of course, patience and practice will help tremendously, as will the additional tools and materials described in this chapter, but you won't need much to start.

Take a good look at the items in the list that follows. The ones marked with • are crucial. The others are helpful, but if your pocketbook or wallet is empty this month, don't worry. Remind yourself, instead, of the quillers who once worked with little more than a feather quill.

- • Quilling tool (select one)
  - Needle tool
  - Slotted quilling tool
  - Hat pin
- • Quilling board

  Quilling designer/board
- • Ruler
- • Pencil

  Compass

  Protractor

  Graph paper
- • Straight pins

  Fringing tools
- • Quilling paper
- • Small, sharp-pointed scissors

  Fine-pointed tweezers
- • Clear-drying, white craft glue
- • Tissues

  Patterns

  Tracing paper

Tools and Materials

Quilling Tools

Quilling paper is usually rolled with either a needle tool or a slotted quilling tool. These are available at craft stores or through quilling suppliers. Choose either tool; each has its advantages. A hat pin will also work well.

The needle tool consists of a long needle that is set into a handle. Circles and scrolls are made by rolling paper strips around the needle. This tool also makes a convenient applicator for the tiny amounts of glue that you'll apply as you glue shapes closed and as you assemble your designs. Be sure to wipe all the glue from the tool's tip with a piece of tissue paper before you roll another strip of paper; glue will wreak havoc with the strips.

Unlike the needle tool, the slotted quilling tool has a slot in its end. Because the slot catches and holds the end of the paper strip, learning to roll circles with this simple tool couldn't be any easier. The needle tool, however, won't leave as large a hole in the center of a rolled shape and won't bend the very end of the paper strip, as the slotted tool does.

The shapes at the top were rolled on the tip of a needle tool, the one in the center was rolled on the needle's center, and those on the bottom were rolled with a slotted quilling tool. Note the difference in hole sizes.

Quilling Board

A handmade quilling board takes just a few minutes to construct. Find a piece of corrugated cardboard with one smooth side; it should be larger than the pattern you intend to quill. A 9" x 12" piece will work well for almost all patterns, though smaller boards are sometimes more convenient.

Cover the cardboard's smooth surface with a sheet of white paper. Next, wrap a piece of waxed paper over the white sheet. When you're ready to start quilling, slip a traced copy of your pattern between the white paper and the waxed paper, where it will be clearly visible. Then assemble and glue together the individual quilled shapes right on top of the waxed paper. If your finished project sticks to the waxed surface, just loosen it with the tip of your needle tool.

Quilling Designer/Board

This board can't be handmade, but it's inexpensive and well worth purchasing. On its upper surface are a series of circular molds in six different sizes as well as a triangular mold to hold your straight pins. The circular molds provide a sure-fire way to quill uniform loose circles, especially important when you want to make eccentric shapes that are uniform in size. (See the "Eccentric Shapes" section on pages 25-26 for further instructions.)

The patterns in this book usually require a standard length of paper for each different size of mold. The smallest mold accepts a 3" length; the largest accepts an 18" length; and the sizes between accept 6", 9", 12", and 15" lengths. You might want to label your board with these sizes until you're so familiar with them that you don't need reminders. And by all means experiment with different lengths of paper; shorter ones will produce rolls that are more open, and longer lengths will yield denser rolls.

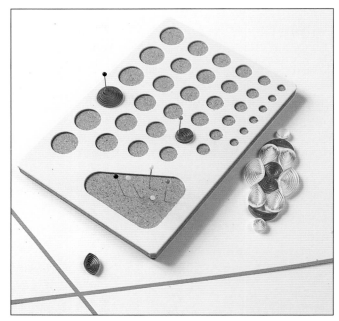

The board's back can be used as an ordinary quilling board; just cover its cork surface with waxed paper.

Ruler, Pencil, Compass, Protractor, and Graph Paper

The project instructions in this book specify the length of each paper strip that's required, so you'll use a ruler frequently. (If you misplace your own, or if you'd like to convert imperial measurements to metric measurements, use the conversion ruler printed on pages 17 and 143.)

These items will also come in handy when you're constructing geometric projects such as snowflakes. You'll use them to create a pattern grid on which to assemble your design.

To make the grid, use your compass to draw several equidistant, concentric circles on a sheet

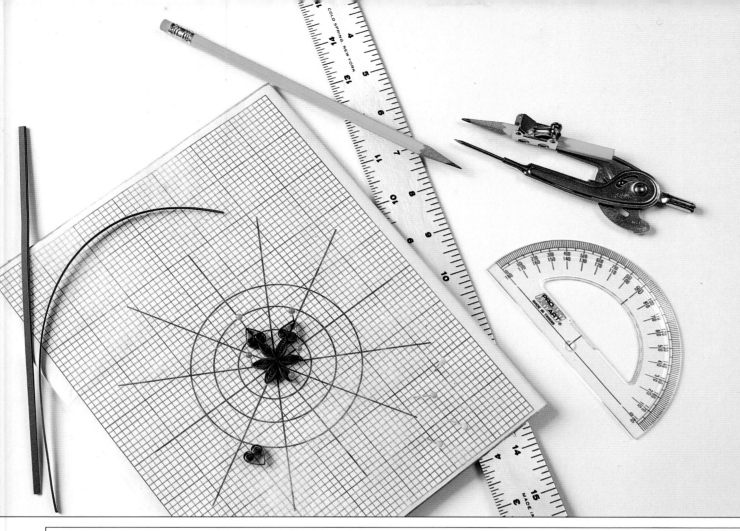

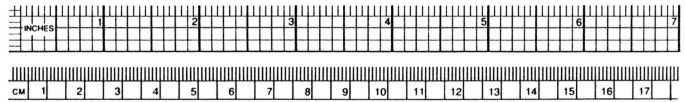

of graph paper. Then use your pencil, ruler, and protractor to bisect the circles with equally spaced lines. Slip the grid behind the waxed paper of your pattern board. By using the circles and lines as guides when you arrange individual shapes, you'll end up with a design that is perfectly aligned.

Graph paper will also prove useful when you weave strips of paper (see "Weaving Paper" on page 29). Purchase sheets that have eight squares per inch; the 1/8" sections will work well when you're weaving 1/8"-wide quilling strips.

Straight Pins

Straight pins serve to hold individual shapes to the handmade quilling board and to hold the centers of eccentric shapes in position on the quilling designer/board while the glue is drying. Pins with round, plastic heads are easy to grasp—and easy to find when you drop them!

Fringing Tools

While it's entirely possible to fringe a strip of paper by cutting tiny slices in one long edge with a pair of scissors, fringing tools do the same job in a fraction of the time. They also make cuts that are uniform in size. Two models are available through quilling suppliers. One cuts a fringe at a 90-degree angle on one edge of either 1/4"-wide or 3/8"-wide paper. The other cuts a fringe at a 45-degree angle along both edges of a 3/8"-wide paper strip that has been folded along its length. The angled cuts this fringer makes are perfect for leaf shapes.

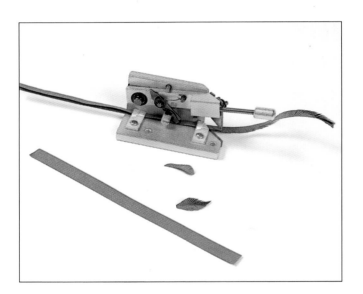

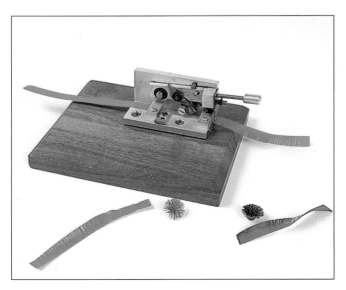

Quilling Paper

In centuries past, quillers cut their strips by hand. Today, though some quillers maintain this tradition, craft shops and quilling suppliers sell inexpensive, pre-cut, packaged strips. These come in various widths and colors and will yield more consistent designs than hand-cut papers. Strips sold in the United States are typically 24" in length, and the most frequently used width is 1/8". Paper strips wider than 3/8" are rarely quilled; they're more often used for fringed flowers, cut-outs, and twisted loops.

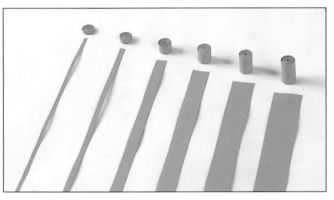

Paper widths, from left to right: narrow (a bit wider than 1/16"), 1/8", 1/4", 3/8", 1/2", and 5/8".

High-quality quilling paper is neither too light nor too heavy; it rolls smoothly, opens evenly, and holds its shape well. It also resists fading, but do avoid displaying quilled projects in direct sunlight. Papers that are too light in weight won't spring open, and poor-quality papers won't roll well.

It's possible to gild the edges of quilling paper with brush-applied metallic paint or spray paints. During this process, lengths of paper are stretched out on edge and held in place by boards on either side. Hobbyists, however, may find that a simpler way to incorporate silver and gold metallic accents is to use quill trim, an attractive paper one side of which is silver or gold in color. Quill trim is rarely rolled except to make fringed flowers and bell shapes.

Another paper variety is parchment, which comes in a number of delicate, pastel colors and gives quilling an entirely different look.

Ingenious quillers have come up with a number of ways to store their paper. One of the easiest is to keep the lengths in handmade, cardboard boxes, each approximately 3" x 3" x 25". Add dividers if you're dealing with only small quantities of paper. Store the strips by width, and be careful not to damage them as you rummage through the boxes in search of a particular color.

Storing paper on a special stand.

Here are two hints regarding paper strips. When you're measuring a strip with which you'll be making a shape that is glued to itself (a tight circle, for example), tear the strip off at the required length—don't cut it. A torn end will glue down much more smoothly than a blunt, cut one. And when you first detach a full-length strip from a multi-strip packet, tear off both its ends. These have been bonded to the other strips' ends; you don't want any of the gummy bond to remain on the strip when you roll it.

Scissors
For trimming excess paper and cutting intricate shapes, a pair of small, sharp-pointed scissors is the tool of choice. Scissors are also used to cut fringes.

Tweezers
Fine-pointed tweezers make a great substitute for fingers when you're positioning tiny shapes during assembly, adjusting coils in loose circles and eccentric shapes, and rearranging stray fringes.

Clear-Drying, White Craft Glue and Tissues
The appearance of even the most perfectly shaped and assembled quillwork may be ruined by visible glue, so be sure you purchase a glue that is colorless when it dries. Avoid the common white glues that are sold for household repairs and woodworking; these are too thick.

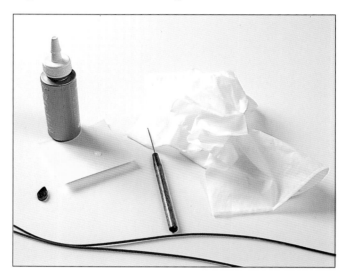

The cardinal rule for using glue is to apply only as much as is necessary—a very small amount indeed! To keep the glue in the bottle from drying out, squeeze just a few drops onto a small square of paper. Then dip your applicator (the tip of a needle tool or a toothpick) into those drops, as needed. Keep your applicator clean by wiping it off with a piece of tissue paper each time you use it .

Patterns
The patterns in this book are designed to help you make the projects' individual shapes and fit them together. In some projects, you'll find only patterns for composite parts of the design, rather than a pattern for the entire design; just use the photograph as a guide when you assemble the various parts. For geometric projects,

only one segment of the pattern may be provided; construct that section as many times as necessary to complete the whole design.

There are two ways to quill from patterns; each of them works best in different situations. In the first of these methods, each roll or scroll is glued in place as soon as it's made. One advantage of this system is that you don't have to worry about storing lots of tiny shapes. You can also adjust shapes to fit an outline as you fill it in. (If all the shapes were made first, you'd probably need to re-shape a few as you reached the outline's edges.)

The second method calls for making all the necessary shapes first and then gluing them together. The advantage to this method is that you can match the shapes' sizes by selecting from among a large number of repeated shapes. If you were making two teardrop flowers, for example, you'd sort through all the teardrops you'd made and select the five or six smallest for one flower's petals and the five or six largest for the other's.

Tracing Paper
Instead of trying to create intricate designs with the tattered remnants of what was once your favorite pattern, you'll want to trace original patterns and use the copies as you work.

Shadow Boxes
Though quillwork looks attractive in a wide variety of frames, shadow boxes will accentuate the depth, dimension, and character of your designs. Their glass will also protect your quillwork from dust. These two-part frames can be made by combining two separate moldings, a technique with which many professional framers are familiar. The explanation and illustrations that follow are ones that you might want to bring to your local frame shop when you're ready to frame your first finished project.

Fig. 1 portrays a typical shadow-box molding. While this type of molding is adequate, it's not the best for quillwork. The molding's inner sides are straight, so your quillwork may look "buried" behind the glass.

Fig. 2 shows a molding the inner surfaces of which flair outward toward the glass. To make a shadow box that won't smother your quillwork, combine this molding with the one shown in Fig. 3. When the two moldings are assembled (see Fig. 4), the glass is held in place between them, and the quillwork rests beneath the lower of the two. If you like, you can add a third molding (see Fig. 5) for added dimension.

When you select moldings, be sure that the distance between the glass and your quillwork (Dimension A) is suitable for your project. Quillwork that consists of only one layer of narrow or 1/8"-wide paper can be placed in a shallow shadow box, but a project that is layered or three-dimensional will require a fairly deep recess in order to look its best.

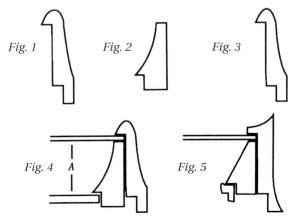

Fig. 1   Fig. 2   Fig. 3

Fig. 4   A   Fig. 5

Rolls

Scrolls

Eccentric Rolls

Techniques and Shapes

Quilled designs are made up of individual shapes, some of them standard and others irregular. Though the names of standard shapes may vary from one published set of instructions to another, the shapes themselves are always formed in the same way. Whether a shape is called a loose circle or a loose coil, for example, doesn't influence how it's made. A complete list of the most common standard shapes (and directions for making each of them) follows this section.

Irregular (or non-standard) shapes are tailor-made by the designer. Because these sponta-neously created shapes don't have names, when a project makes use of them, the pattern and photograph provided with that project become especially important. You can't turn to a stan-dard set of directions when irregular shapes are called for, but patterns and photos will help you decide how to create the shapes portrayed.

Before you tackle your first project, practice making a few of the standard shapes that follow. Use 4" lengths of 1/8"-wide paper.

Rolls
Tight Circle
The very simplest standard shape, often used to make a flower center or bud, is a tight circle.

To roll a tight circle with a needle tool or hat pin, first tear off a strip of paper to the length specified in the instructions. Moisten one end of the strip slightly, and place that end against your index finger. Position the tool on the end of the paper, and press the paper around the tool with your thumb. Roll the

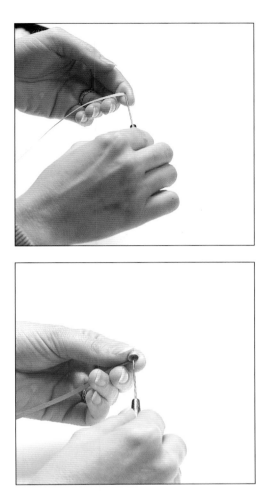

ing. Apply a small amount of glue to the strip's end, press the end in place against the side of the roll, and hold the shape until the glue adheres.

When you're first learning to use the needle tool, roll each strip on the center of the needle. After you've become proficient, you may want to use the tool's tip instead; it will leave a smaller hole in the roll's center.

To make a tight circle with a slotted quilling tool, first thread the paper into the tool's slot. Adjust the slot's position so that the strip's end is just at the slot's edge, and then turn the tool so that the paper wraps around it in a circular motion. The slot will grasp the paper's end tightly. Remove the roll by gently slipping the tool from the roll's center and gluing the strip's end in place.

paper without turning the tool, keeping the strip's edges as even as possible. Slip the needle from the roll's center, grasping the roll with your fingers to keep it from unwind-

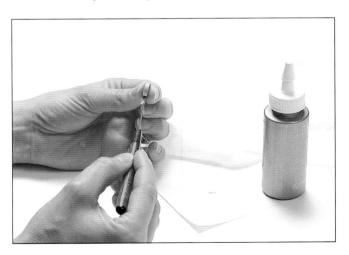

Loose Circle
Perhaps the most common standard shape, one which is made and then pinched to form other shapes, is the loose circle. To make a loose circle, first use a quilling tool to roll a tight circle, but don't glue the circle closed. Slip it off the tool, place it on a flat surface, and let its coils expand. If the outer coils stick together, adjust them by turning the center coils to tighten

them slightly, drawing the outer coils in toward the center. Once the circle has expanded, glue its end in place.

When a pattern calls for many loose circles (or shapes made with them), a quilling designer/board is helpful. Tight circles placed into one of the board's molds will expand to the mold's exact size. Provided that your circles are made with equal lengths of paper, they'll all be the same size.

Teardrop
Roll and glue a loose circle. Then pinch one side of the circle to a point.

Shaped Teardrop
Roll and glue a loose circle, pinch one side into a point, and curl the point in one direction.

Marquise
Roll and glue a loose circle, and then pinch it on opposite sides.

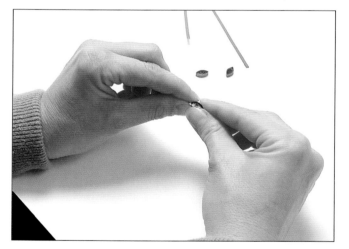

Shaped Marquise
Make a marquise, and then curl its two pinched points in opposite directions.

Crescent
Make a teardrop. Then pinch another point, one that is not quite opposite to the first point. Curl the two points toward one another.

Square
Make a marquise. Then turn it ninety degrees and pinch it again on two opposite sides; the four pinched points should be equidistant from one another.

Rectangle
Make a marquise, turn it slightly, and pinch it again on two opposite sides.

Triangle
Roll and glue a loose circle. Pinch three points simultaneously by pressing the circle between the thumb and forefinger of one hand and pushing it against the side of one finger on the other hand.

Bunny Ear
Roll and glue a loose circle. Then make a rounded indentation on one side. (Note that this shape is similar to the crescent, but its points are closer together.)

Half Circle
Roll and glue a loose circle. Flatten one side by pinching the circle at two points.

Rolled Heart (Arrow)
Roll and glue a loose circle. Pinch a point on one side. Then make a sharp indentation on the opposite side. Be sure that all three points are very sharp.

Holly Leaf
Roll and glue a loose circle. Pinch five or six points, making a rounded indentation between each set of two points.

Scrolls
Loose Scroll
Roll one end of the strip, leaving the other end loose.

Open Heart

Crease the strip at its center. Then roll each end in toward the crease.

V Scroll

Crease a length of paper at its center. Then roll each end toward the outside. To make a closed V scroll, glue the inner surfaces of the folded section together.

S Scroll

Roll one end of the strip toward the strip's center. Then roll the other end toward the center to make an S shape.

C Scroll

Roll both ends of the strip toward the strip's center.

Variations of Scrolls

These are made by rolling one end of the strip to a point that is off-center.

Double Scroll

Tear two lengths of paper, one shorter than the other. (Lengths may be specified in the instructions.) Rest the two strips on top of one another, with one end of the shorter length 1/4" from the end of the longer length. Glue the strips together at this overlapping point. Roll the double strip, starting with the end that has the longer strip on the outside. Release the tension on the roll, and then pull slightly on the shorter length to separate the coiled strips. Glue the ends together.

Double Scroll with Flag

Fold a length of paper in half. Starting from the two loose ends, roll the folded strip; the inside strip will form a flag (or loop) near the crease.

Triple Scroll

Fold a length of paper in half. Roll each end just a few turns. Then roll the folded end down to meet the first two coils.

Connected Scrolls

Roll several loose scrolls. Curve the unrolled ends away from the rolled ends. Then position one roll next to another by curving the loose end of one shape around the rolled end of the next shape. Glue each scroll to the one next to it.

Eccentric Shapes

Eccentric shapes (not to be confused with irregular shapes) are ones with centers that have been pulled to one side. Unlike the center of a typical loose circle, which remains in the circle's middle, the center of an eccentric circle is pulled toward one edge of the circle and glued in place. A quilling designer/board makes this job especially easy.

Eccentric Loose Circle

All eccentric shapes are made with eccentric loose circles. Start by rolling a tight circle and placing it in the quilling designer/board. When the circle has expanded, glue its end in place. Then hook a straight pin through its center, and move the center to the mold's edge. To keep the center in this position, push the pin into the board. Place a small amount of glue on top of the circle, on the area between the pin and the mold's edge. Rub the glue in well so that it will spread between the rolled layers. Let the glue dry. Before you remove the pin, twist it to loosen any glue that may be stuck to it.

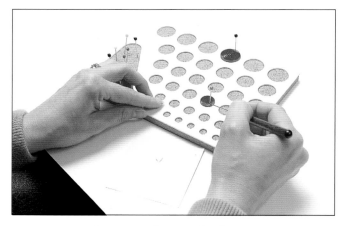

Once you've made the eccentric loose circle, you'll create the desired shape by pinching or curling it just as you do when making shapes that aren't eccentric. There's one crucial difference between an eccentric shape and any other, however; an eccentric shape should always be turned upside down when you display it because glue will be visible on the other surface. (When eccentric shapes are shown in patterns, their "centers" are indicated by dots.)

Eccentric Teardrop

Hold the glued section between your thumb and forefinger. With your other thumb and forefinger, pinch the opposite side to make a point. The more coils you include when you pinch the shape, the sharper this point will be.

Eccentric Marquise

Make two points by pinching two opposite sides of the circle, making sure that the glued portion is between these two points. The more coils you pinch, the more slender your marquise will be.

Eccentric Fan

First, shape an eccentric marquise. Then, holding each point between a thumb and forefinger, press in on the same side of each point, expanding the coils on one side of the marquise.

Eccentric Crescent

Pinch the loose circle at two points that are not exactly opposite one another. Then curl the ends toward one another. Apply glue across the shape's center, and hold the shape until the glue dries.

Eccentric Bunny Ear

Make a rounded indentation on one side of the eccentric loose circle, and then pinch two sharp points.

Eccentric Tulip

Shape an eccentric marquise. Then pinch another point on one side. Push the two sections between these three points inward; then push the three points together.

Other Shaping Techniques
Fringed Flower
Paper is fringed with either scissors or one of the two fringing tools described on page 18. If you use scissors, keep in mind that the closer the cuts are to each other, the more attractive the flower will be.

Fringe a length of paper along one side. Roll the fringed paper into a tight circle, and glue the circle closed. With your fingernail, spread the fringes so that they open up from the roll's center. Use your needle tool to curl the outermost ring of fringes.

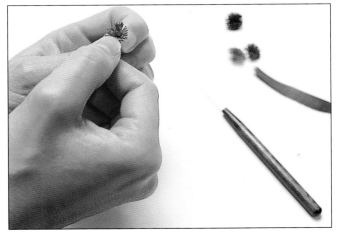

Fringed Flower with Center

Select two widths of paper, one wider than the other (3/8" and 1/8", for example). Fringe the wider strip, and then glue the narrower strip to one end of it. Begin rolling with the narrower paper, which will be the flower's center, and continue rolling until both widths form a single tight circle. Glue the circle closed, and open the fringed section with your fingernail.

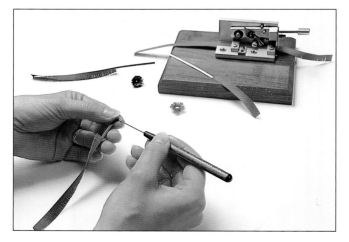

Duo-Tone Fringed Flower

Select two different colors of paper, and fringe a length of each. Place one fringed strip on top of the other, and roll both into a single tight circle. Glue the circle closed, and spread the fringed edges with your fingernail.

Grape Roll

Roll and glue a tight circle. Gently push the center of the circle out to make a conical roll. Then, either spread a thin layer of glue on the concave (inner) surface to help the roll maintain its

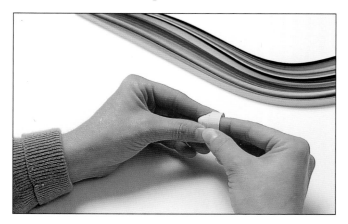

shape, or apply the glue to the convex (outer) surface if the concave side will be displayed. Let the glue dry completely.

Grape rolls are made with rounded, pointed, or flat ends. Grapes and berries should be just slightly rounded; bells have a more pronounced point at their ends. To make a flower pot, flatten the extended center section before applying glue to the inner surface.

Spiral

Position one end of the paper length on the quilling tool by placing it an angle. Roll the strip down the tool to make a spiral, keeping a little tension on it with the thumb and forefinger of your tool-holding hand as you do. When you reach the needle's base, let the starting end of the spiral slip off the needle while you continue to roll.

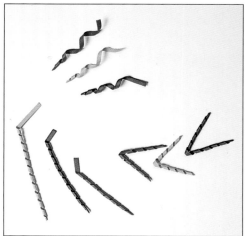

Regular spirals are rolled tightly. To make a loose spiral, first roll a tight spiral and remove it from the tool. Run the side of the needle down the inside of the paper length, from the loose end toward the tight end, as if you were curling a piece of ribbon with a scissors' blade. Stop just before you get to the spiral's tight end so that you won't take all the tension out of its point. Double spirals, which are V-shaped, are made by rolling from each end of the strip.

Loop Method

Make a small, circular loop, and glue it at the bottom. Continue making loops, each one larger than the one before, pinching them together as you shape each one. To hold the loops together, apply glue to one side of the pinched end, holding the end until the glue dries.

Pegs

Pegs consist of one or more tight circles that are glued to the back of design sections in order to raise them away from the background. For added height, make double pegs by gluing one peg to another.

Weaving Paper

Slip a piece of graph paper under the waxed paper on the quilling board. Position lengths of paper horizontally, using the graph lines as guides and pinning one end of each length to the board. Then weave lengths of paper vertically through the pinned strips, gluing the strips together at each point where a horizontal length crosses a vertical length. When the glue has dried, unpin the completed piece, and trim it to the desired size.

Twisted Loop

This loop can be made with paper of any width. Cut a short length, overlap its ends, and glue the ends together to form a tight, pointed loop. Then trim the excess from the overlapped ends.

To ensure twisted loops of equal sizes, twist each one so that the pointed loop is in the strip's center and the two squared ends meet in a point as well.

Huskings

Huskings are shapes made by winding paper around a series of pins. Contemporary English quiller, Brenda Rhodes, has experimented extensively with them and has written a booklet entitled *Huskings: An Exploration of an Old Technique.*

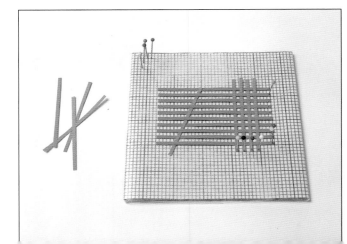

The shield-shaped fire screen (see page 8) illustrates some of the many ways in which huskings can be used—as flower petals, incorporated in baskets, and included in borders.

To make a straight husking, arrange four straight pins on your quilling board as shown in the diagram. Begin by wrapping a length of paper around Pins 1 and 2; glue the paper where it overlaps at Pin 1. Then continue by wrapping around Pin 3, back around Pin 1, around Pin 4, back around Pin 1, around Pin 5, and back to Pin 1. Tear off the excess paper, and glue it in place. Pinch the loops into points or leave them rounded. You may vary the number of pins you use and the distances at which they're spaced.

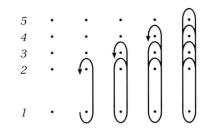

Fan-shaped huskings are made in a similar fashion, but the pins are positioned differently. For added stability, you may want to wind around Pins 1 and 2 twice. Also, glue the paper periodically. If you'd like to make a collar (not all fan-shaped huskings have one), wind several loops around the husking's exterior before gluing the strip's end in place. Add a dot of glue at the Pin 1 position before removing the pins. To make huskings of uniform size, replace all the pins in the same holes.

The most popular huskings today are straight and fan shapes, but there's no limit to the number of different shapes and sizes that huskings can take. Just vary the positions in which you place your pins.

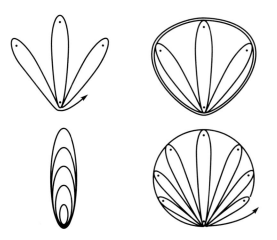

Folded Roses
Using a slotted quilling tool, first slip the end of the strip into the slot. Begin rolling the strip to make a center for the flower. Next, fold the paper away from you at a right angle. Roll the paper again, keeping the bottom edge tight on the tool while allowing the paper's top edge to flare outward. Continue rolling until the fold is on the top. Make another right-angled fold, and roll the paper again while allowing it to flare out. Repeat the folding and rolling steps until the entire strip has been shaped, or until the rose is the size that you desire. Glue the end in place.

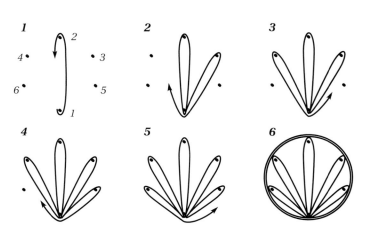

end into a rounded point, and cut a slit on the other end. Curl about 3/16" of the rounded end, using the quilling tool's side. Hold the petal with this curled side down, and overlap the two sections on the slotted end. Glue them together to form a petal with its curled end facing outward and slightly raised.

Position the slotted ends of two petals together, opposite to each other, and glue them together. Place two more petals between the first two. Add four petals under and between the first four. Then glue six petals under these eight to make the outermost layer.

Curled Flower
(with rounded petals, rolled inward)
Follow the instructions for the curled flower just described, but roll the curl forward, toward the flower's center. Use only four petals for the center and six for the outermost layer.

Curled Flower
(made using rectangles)
Cut a 1/2" length of 3/8"-wide paper. Using the side of the quilling tool, curl the two corners of one end, and cut a slit in the other end. Hold the petal with its curled side down, and overlap the two pieces on the slotted end, gluing them together to form a petal with its curled end raised. For the center section, glue five petals together, with each petal slightly overlapping the next. Glue five petals underneath these five to make the outermost layer.

Curled Flower
(with rounded petals, rolled outward)
Cut a 5/8" length of 3/8"-wide paper. Trim one

A Project for Practice

Quilling can be as simple or complex, serious or playful, quick or time-consuming as you desire. If your leisure hours are few, don't despair. Just select small designs that call for basic shapes such as loose and tight circles, marquises, and teardrops. These standard shapes can be transformed into truly impressive projects. If, on the other hand, your life's goal is to create a quilled mural for the living room wall, and you have the time to spare, go right ahead. You won't need any extras except more than the usual amount of paper and patience!

The project that follows will prepare you for those in the next chapter. It's a fairly easy one that makes use of only six shapes, five of them standard and one hand-cut. Relax and take your time; if you need a reminder at any stage, just refer back to the information in earlier parts of this chapter. Once you get a feel for how basic shapes are rolled, glued, and assembled, there won't be any stopping you.

Before you start, assemble your tools and materials. You'll need a quilling tool, glue, a ruler, a handmade quilling board, straight pins, a tracing of the pattern, a pair of scissors, and a sheet of parchment to serve as a background. Of course, you'll need paper, too; glance through the instructions that follow to find out which colors and widths are required.

Next, be sure to wash your hands. Oil or dirt on your fingertips may discolor your paper shapes. Keep a few tissues nearby; use them to wipe any glue from your hands and your needle tool.

Slip the copy of the pattern behind the quilling board's waxed paper. Read the instructions next. You'll notice that they are divided into sections, each of which represents a part of the total design. Note that the lengths given represent the lengths of the paper strips, not the lengths or widths of rolled shapes. A 6" marquise, for example, is made with a 6"-long paper strip.

You're ready to get started!

Beginner's Floral Design
Use 1/8"-wide paper unless another width is specified.

Marquise Flowers (make two)
Make seven brick 6" marquises, and glue them together.
Add a pale dusty rose 3" tight circle for the flower's center.
Make a stem by gluing a short length of green paper (on its edge) to the flower.

Teardrop Flower
Glue together five dusty rose 4" teardrops.
Add a brick 2" tight circle for the flower's center.
Make a stem by adding a short length of green paper.

Flower Buds (make two)
Glue a pale dusty rose 3" teardrop into a soft ivory 3" V scroll.
Add a short length of green paper as a stem.

Quilled Leaves (make three)
Roll a green 3" teardrop.

Cut-Out Leaves (make two)
With a pair of scissors, cut a leaf shape from pale green paper, and curl it slightly.

• Assembly
Glue the uppermost, large marquise flower to the background.
Roll a brick 3" tight circle to serve as a peg, and glue it to the back of the other marquise flower.
Then position this flower, and glue the peg to the background.
Glue the flower-and-bud assemblies to the background.
Add the quilled and cut-out leaves.
Your design is finished! If you wish to frame it, cut a circular opening in a piece of complementary mat board, and insert the mat board and design into a frame.

The Projects

Berries

Berry designs, with their promise of plenty, are a natural for the kitchen. This selection looks lovely framed, but if you'd rather make individual refrigerator magnets like those in the photo, take a look at the project on pages 97 and 98.

Use narrow paper for all parts of these designs.

Raspberries

Berries (make four)
Glue together seven raspberry 4" tight circles to make the lower layer.
Make an upper layer by adding three raspberry 4" tight circles.
Add narrow, short, pointed lengths of green paper to create the calyxes.

 Leaves (make six)
Glue together three green 3" marquises for each leaf.

Stems
Glue together short lengths of green paper so that they'll stand on edge.

Strawberries

Berries (make two)
Fill in the berry outlines with red 1-1/2" loose circles.
Add four or five green 1-1/2" marquises to make the calyxes.

 Leaves (make four)
Glue together eight green 3" marquises to make each leaf.

Stems
Glue together short lengths of green paper, on edge.

Blackberries

Berries (make three)
Glue together ten black 3" tight circles for the lower layer.
Add four black 3" tight circles for the upper layer.
Cut narrow, short, pointed lengths of green paper, and add them to create the calyxes.

 Leaves (make six)
Glue together three green 3" marquises to make each leaf.

Stems
Glue together short lengths of green paper, on edge.

• Assembly
Glue the berries and leaves to the stems. (For added dimension, glue some of the leaves at slight angles.)
Position the berry-leaf combinations on tan parchment paper, and glue them in place

Kitchen Herbs

From gourmet dining establishments to humble cottage kitchens, herbs transform everyday food into feasts. Chefs around the world treasure the three herbs portrayed in these life-like quilled replicas. Display them on a kitchen wall, or give them to a friend who loves to cook.

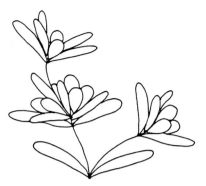

Rosemary

Dill (Top Layer)

Dill (Bottom Layer)

Use narrow paper for all three designs.

Rosemary

To make the flowers, roll eleven sky blue 2" teardrops.

To make the two-loop, three-loop, and four-loop leaves, first review the instructions and diagrams for making straight huskings (see pages 29-30). Then arrange a five-pin, straight huskings form. Place Pins 1 and 2 so that they're 1/4" apart; Pins 2 and 3, 3 and 4, and 4 and 5 should be 1/8" apart.

Make eight green two-loop huskings, eight green three-loop huskings, and two green four-loop huskings.

Cut two short lengths of green paper for the stems.

• Assembly

Using the assembly pattern, position the flowers, leaves, and stems. Avoid gluing all of the leaves flat; to add depth to the design, elevate the tips of several. The very top group has one flower and four leaves on the lower layer and one flower and one leaf on the upper layer. The group below has four flowers and four leaves on the lower layer and two flowers and three leaves on the upper layer. The group on the right has two flowers and three leaves on the lower layer and one flower and one leaf on the upper layer. Add the two four-loop leaves at the point where the two stems meet.

Dill

To make the flowers, roll twenty-four yellow 2" teardrops. Glue these together in clusters of three, and attach a short green stem to each cluster.

Make the feathery dill leaves by gluing together short lengths of green paper that are slightly curled on one end.

• Assembly

As you assemble this design, note that there are three layers in it: a bottom layer of flowers, stems, and leaves; a middle layer of flowers and stems; and a top layer of leaves (portrayed separately in the patterns).

First arrange the flower clusters in two layers, placing five on the bottom layer and three on the top layer.

Glue the short stems of the clusters to one longer stem of green paper.

Add the two lowest sets of leaves.

Glue the top layer of leaves to the main stem (an arrow in the pattern marks this spot). This leaf layer should partially cover the flowers.

Tarragon

To make buds, roll eighteen pale
green 2" tight circles.

To make leaves, roll six green 2"
shaped marquises and eight
green 3" shaped marquises.

• Assembly

Cut lengths of green paper for
the three stems, and glue
them together.

Glue two 2" leaves to the ends
of each stem.

Glue four buds together, and
then glue the assembled buds
between the 2" leaves.

To make a second layer, glue
two buds on top of the four
grouped buds.

Position the remaining leaves,
and glue them to the stem.

Tarragon

Rosemary

Dill

Tarragon

Sailboats

Their billowing sails make these two boats come alive. Can't you feel the fresh breeze blowing behind them? Frame these pieces, or quill them as ornaments for a tree or sunny window.

Use 1/8"-wide paper unless another width is specified.

Sailboat Number One

Hull
Fill in the outline with red 3" squares and triangles.

Sails
Fill in the outlines with white 3" marquises.
Gently round and shape the jib so that it will billow out.

Flag
Cut a triangular flag from deep blue 1/4"-wide paper.
To make the flag's stripe, cut a narrow length, with one pointed end, from red paper; then center and glue it on the triangle.

• Assembly
Paint or stain a length of 1/8" dowel for the mast.
Glue the mainsail to the mast, the mast to the hull, the jib to mast, and the flag to the mast's top.

Sailboat Number Two

Hull
Fill in the outline with dark green 3" squares and triangles.

Sails
Fill in the outlines with white 3" marquises.
Gently round and shape the jibs so that they'll billow out.

* Assembly
To make the mast, cut a length of 1/8" dowel, and paint or stain it.

Glue the mainsail to the mast
and the mast to the hull.
Position the jib that goes closest
to the mast, and glue it in
place.
Glue a short, folded length of
paper around the top marquise
on the other jib, fitting the
marquise into the V-shaped
fold.
Position and glue this jib so that it
overlaps the other one, gluing
the top of its V-shaped strip to
the top of the other sail.

Number One

Number Two

Grapevine Wreath

As autumn leaves begin to turn, what could be more appropriate than a quilled wreath, decorated in traditional fall colors? For that matter, why not make a wreath for every season? All you'll need to do is vary your color selections.

Vine bases are available from florists, craft stores, and many discount marts.

Large Flower

Using 1/2"-wide gold paper, make twelve 2-1/2" twisted loops.

Glue six of these together to make the center section, placing each loop at an angle, with its flat, pointed end slightly elevated.

Add the six outer loops; these are arranged flat.

Medium Flowers (make two orange and one persimmon)

Using 3/8"-wide paper, make twelve 2" twisted loops.

Glue six loops together for the center section, angling them as you did when you made the large flower.

Add the six outer loops, once again placing them in a flat position.

Small Flowers (make two yellow, two apricot, and one rust)

Using 3/8"-wide paper, make twelve 1-1/2" twisted loops.

Glue four together for the center section, angling them as explained previously.

Add the eight outer loops, just as you did for the other flowers.

Leaves (make seven)

Using green 3/8"-wide paper, make three 2" twisted loops, and glue them together.

• Assembly

Position and wire a bow to the wreath.

Bend a piece of floral wire into a U shape, and glue it to the back of the large flower.

Glue a narrow strip of paper over the wire to secure the wire to the flower's back.

To elevate this flower on the wreath, cut a small block of foam backing, and run the wire through the foam so that the foam rests in the center of the flower's back.

Fasten the large flower above the bow.

Arrange the other flowers on the wreath and bow, and glue the ones on the bow in place.

Use wire to attach the other flowers to the wreath. Twist the wires to secure them, and clip off the excess. (You may want to glue some sets of two flowers together before wiring them in place.)

Glue the leaves to the flowers.

Bird Shalom

In this distinctive design, a dove of peace flies above the Hebrew word shalom, *which means welcome and peace. The Hebrew letters (*shin, lamed, vav, *and* final mem*) are written from right to left, and the colors, white and blue, are the colors of the Israeli flag. While the design fits well in a 5" x 7" shadowbox frame, you may also center it on an 8" x 10" background and double-mat it.*

Use 1/8"-wide white quilling paper for the entire design. Let the patterns guide you as you make this project's irregular shapes.

Border

Measure and cut a 5" x 7" piece of mat board.
Measure 3/8" in from each edge of the mat board, and lightly mark four lines.
Glue lengths of quilling paper just inside these lines.

Letters

shin

Make the three uppermost sections of the letter with three 4-1/2" shaped marquises.
Make the three center shapes from three 3" marquises.
For the lowest section, make a 7-1/2" rectangle.
Glue these seven pieces together, using the pattern as a guide.

lamed

Make one shaped marquise with a 4-1/2" length of quilling paper.
Make two shaped marquises with 8" lengths.
Glue the three shapes together.

vav

Make the upper shaped marquise with a 4-1/2" length of paper.
Make the lower marquise with a 6" length.
Glue the two shapes together.

final mem

To make the upper shape, first make a rectangle with an 8" length of paper; then curl one of its corners.
Make the rectangle on the bottom with a 7-1/2" length.
Create the two sides by shaping two slender marquises from 3" lengths.
Glue all four pieces together.

• Assembly of Letters

Using the photograph as a guide, glue the four letters in place on the mat.

Bird

To make the wings, roll and shape two 8" loose circles as shown in the pattern.
Make the body by shaping a 17" loose circle.
The head is a 4-1/2" teardrop.
Glue all four pieces together, and then glue the bird to the mat.

Scrolls

Cut two lengths of paper, curve them as shown in the photograph, and glue them on edge to the mat. The longer of the two should run from the top of lamed to the underside of the bird, and the shorter length should extend above lamed.

final mem   *vav*   *lamed*   *shin*

Flowers and Butterflies

As two, brightly colored butterflies perch delicately above them, the three miniature gardens in this design spill forth their blossoms. The blend of soothing blues and bright yellows makes this piece especially appropriate for a kitchen breakfast nook.

Use 1/8"-wide paper unless another width is specified. Note that the large flowers are made using a technique called paper sculpture; they're not quilled.

**Sculptured Flowers
(make two large and two small)**
Cut twelve petals from slate blue sculpture paper.
Create ragged edges on each one by fringing it as shown in the patterns. (Make the fringes as narrow as possible.)
Curl the fringed ends backward and the opposite ends forward.
Use scissors or a paper punch to cut a small blue circle.

Sculptured Flowers (large and small)

To make the flower's lower layer, glue the points of six petals to the circle, overlapping each petal slightly.

To create the upper layer, glue the points of another six petals to the lower layer.

To make centers, use narrow paper to roll fifteen to eighteen gold 1/2" loose scrolls. Glue these in a cluster to the middle of the flower.

Bunny Ear Flowers (make eight)

Glue together four bright yellow 5" bunny ears.
Add a soft green 4" tight circle for the flower's center.

Teardrop Flowers (make seven)

Glue together five gold 3" teardrops.
Add a white 1-1/2" loose circle for the center.

Quilled Leaves on Stems (make nine)

Roll two green 3" marquises.
Glue these shapes to a short length of green paper.

Cut-Out Leaves (make nine)

Cut a leaf from green paper. Fringe its edges, and curve the leaf slightly.

Scrolls (make seven)

Roll a green 2" loose scroll.

Butterfly Body (make two)

Using the triangular pattern provided, cut the body shape from a sheet of gold paper.
Roll the triangle from its wide end, and glue it closed. Be sure to keep the roll straight; the point should be in the exact center when you're through.

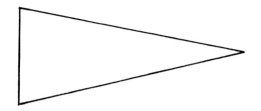

Butterfly Wings (make two large and two small for each butterfly)

Use the loop method to make the wings, winding two loops of each color and gluing each loop in place as you wind it. The colors, beginning with the smallest loop, are yellow, bright yellow, gold, turquoise, and black. Note that the butterfly on the left has slightly smaller wings than the other butterfly.

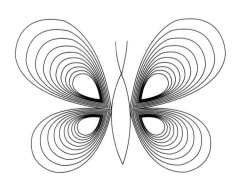

• Assembly

Glue the butterfly wings to the bodies, allowing each wing to dry completely before gluing the next. (The wings on the right-hand butterfly are nearly open, while the wings on the left-hand butterfly are almost closed.)

Make antennae by folding two 1" lengths of narrow black paper and gluing one to each body.

Cut or purchase a 12" x 6-1/2" mat, with three, 3"-diameter, round openings.

Set one bunny ear flower aside, and glue a quilled leaf grouping to each of the other seven.

Glue two leaf groupings to the remaining bunny ear flower.

Glue a scroll to each teardrop flower.

Position the two small sculptured flowers in the center opening and a large sculptured flower in each of the side openings.

Glue these in place, and add the cut-out leaves.

Next, add the bunny ear flowers, placing the one with two leaf groupings in the center design.

Add the teardrop flowers with scrolls.

Position the two butterflies on the mat, as shown in the photo, and glue them in place.

Quilled Wreath

Wreath-making adventures don't depend on vine bases, evergreens, or flowers. Try quilling paper instead; your color choices will never be limited by the time of year or your local climate!

Use 1/8"-wide paper for all parts of this design.

Wreath Base

Using a needle tool or heavy-gauge wire, make three long spirals with two 24" strips of light green paper and one 24" length of medium green paper.

Twist all three spirals together, and shape them into a wreath that's approximately 2-1/2" in diameter.

Folded Roses (make four)

Use a 6" length of sky blue 1/4"-wide paper to make each flower. (For detailed instructions, see page 30.)

Fringed Flower

Use a 2" length of pale dusty rose to make this flower.

Small Rolled Heart Flowers (make five)

To make the twenty flower petals (you'll need four for each of the five flowers), first make twenty strips by gluing 1/2" lengths of one color to 1/2" lengths of another color. Then roll and shape each glued strip into a rolled heart. The list that follows specifies color combinations and the end from which you should start each roll.

Raspberry-White (make eight)
Roll from the white end.

White-Sky Blue (make eight)
Roll from the sky blue end.

Mauve-White (make four)
Roll from the mauve end.

Glue together four petals to make each flower.

Center Flower

To make the center petal, first place a 3" length of mauve paper on top of a 3" length of white paper, and then roll both pieces simultaneously, with the white paper on the outside.

Shape the roll into a marquise.

To make each of the two outer petals, place a mauve 2" length on top of a white 2" length.

Roll these lengths simultaneously, with the white paper on the outside, and then shape the roll into a curved petal.

Glue the two petals to the sides of the marquise.

Bow

Make three circles by gluing together the ends of a 4" raspberry length, the ends of a 2" raspberry length, and the ends of a 3" sky blue length.

To make double loops from each circle, place a small amount of glue at any point on the inside of each one, and then press the circle in half so that the glue fastens one of its sides to the other in the pinched circle's center.

Glue the three double loops together at their glued centers, with the largest at the bottom and the smallest at the top.

Wrap a piece of sky blue paper around the center of the glued loops.

Add two short lengths of sky blue paper, each with an angled end, as streamers.

• Assembly

Glue a 4" x 6" piece of background paper (a scrap of wallpaper makes an attractive background) to the back of a 5" x 7" mat.

Using the photograph as a guide, glue the wreath to the background.

Add the flowers and the bow.

Place the project into a 5" x 7" frame.

Chickadees

Chickadees often appear when ripe autumn berries beckon, but these two quilled versions are guaranteed to become full-time residents in your home.

Use narrow paper to make the birds and 1/8"-wide paper to make the tree limb and berries.

Birds' Bodies (make two; each has its own pattern)

Begin by rolling a black 4" grape roll for the eye.

Wrap a length of white around the eye, and position it on the pattern.

Fill in the numbered areas of both bird patterns as follows:
1. black 2" marquises
2. white 2" marquises
3. pale peach 2" marquises
4. grey 2" marquises

Add a black 1-1/2" triangle for the beak.

Tail Feathers (make five for each bird)

Using the illustration as a guide, first cut a 6" length of grey paper, and mark it at 1-1/4", 2", and 2-3/4".

Then cut a 7-1/8" length of silver grey paper, and mark it at 1-5/8", 2-3/8", and 3-1/8".

Glue the two lengths together at the ends marked A.

Shape the grey 1-1/4" section into a loop.

Shape the 1-5/8" silver grey section into a loop around the grey loop.

Continue shaping each consecutive loop around the last one, ending with the 3-1/8" silver grey loop.

Pinch the loops to flatten them into a feather shape.

To make the tail's lower layer, glue three feathers together.

Add two feathers to make the upper layer.

Glue the assembled layers to the body.

Wings (make two; each has its own pattern)

Fill in the wing patterns with grey 3", 4", 5", and 6" teardrops.

Glue the wings to the bodies.

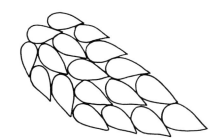

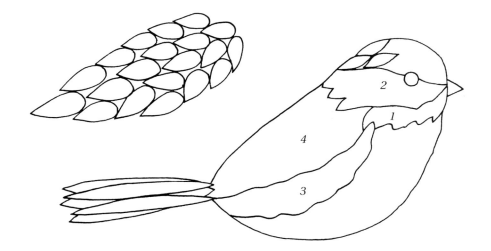

Tail-feather sections
(not actual size)

A	1-1/4"	2"	2-3/4"

A	1-5/8"	2-3/8"	3-1/8"

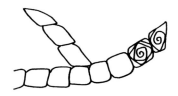

Bluebird in a Dogwood Tree

You can be sure that winter is finally over when your dogwood tree bursts into bloom, and you spot a bluebird among the blossoms.

Tree Limb and Berries

The limb and its branches are made with brown 3" and 4" squares, rectangles, and marquises, some irregularly shaped.

Arrange the limb shapes, and glue them together. The larger shapes should make up the thicker parts of the limb.

Roll approximately forty crimson 4" grape rolls for berries.

Attach these to the branches' tips with short lengths of brown paper.

• Assembly

Using the photograph as a guide, glue the limb and branches to the background.

Add the berries.

Position the birds and glue them in place.

Use 1/8"-wide paper to make the body and tree limb. Make the tail feathers, wings, dogwood blossoms, and leaves with narrow paper.

Bird's Body

Begin by rolling a black 4" grape roll for the eye.

Wrap a length of white paper (twice) around this grape roll, and position the roll on the pattern.

Fill in pattern area 1 with cadet blue 2" marquises.

Make two black irregularly shaped marquises, one 3" for the upper part of the beak and one 3-1/3" for the lower part of the beak.

Glue the beak shapes together, and then glue the beak to the head.

Glue a pale dusty rose 2" crescent directly below the beak.

Add two dusty rose marquises below the crescent, at the top of the area marked 2.

Now fill in the remaining pattern areas as follows:

2. brick 2" marquises
3. dusty rose 2" marquises
4. pale dusty rose 2" marquises
5. white 2" marquises

Tail Feathers (make five)

Using the illustration at the bottom of the next page as a guide, first cut a 9-1/2" length of deep blue paper, and mark four sections on it.

Then cut a 7-1/8" length of cadet blue paper, and mark three sections as shown.

Glue the two lengths together at the ends marked A.

Shape the deep blue 1-1/4" section into a loop.

Shape the 1-5/8" cadet blue section into a loop around the deep blue loop.

Continue shaping each consecutive loop around the last one, ending with the 3-1/2" deep blue section.

Pinch the loops to flatten them into a feather shape.

To make the tail's lower layer, glue three feathers together.

Add two feathers to make the upper layer.

Wing

To make the teardrops and marquises for the wing, use cadet blue lengths ranging from 3" to 9" (in 1" increments). Shape each piece to fit those shown in the wing pattern, using the smaller shapes at the top of the wing. Outline the final nine shapes with a length of black paper.

Glue the completed wing to the body.

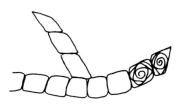

Tree Limb

The limb and its branches are made with brown 3" and 4" squares, rectangles, and marquises. (Note that some are irregularly shaped.) Glue these together, using the larger shapes to construct the thicker parts.

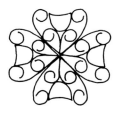

Large Dogwood Blossoms (make three)

To make each petal, glue together a white 2-1/2" bunny ear, a white 2" V scroll, and a white 3" open heart.

To represent the light brown shades of a dogwood blossom, glue a short length (approximately 1/4") of tan paper into the scallop at the outer edge of each petal.

Glue four petals together.

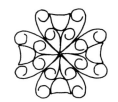 Make a flower center by rolling seven soft green 1" tight circles, gluing them together, and then gluing them to the flower.

Small Dogwood Blossoms (make six)

Make this just as you made the large flower, but use a white 2" bunny ear, a white 1-1/2" V scroll, and a white 2-1/2" open heart. Glue short lengths of tan paper into the scallops. The flower's center is exactly like that of the large flower.

Leaves

Make three leaves by gluing together three green 6" marquises.

Make nine leaves by gluing together three green 4" marquises.

Make thirteen leaves by gluing together three green 3" marquises.

• Assembly

Glue the limb to the background. Add the flowers and leaves. Position the bird, and glue it in place.

Tail-feather sections
(not actual size)

| A | 1-1/4" | 2" | 2-3/4" | 3-1/2" | 9-1/2" |

| A | 1-5/8" | 2-3/8" | 3-1/8" | 7-1/8" |

Old-Fashioned Garden

With its cleverly cut mat border, this garden scene's three-dimensional effect makes the design so realistic that you can almost smell the sweet scents of summer and hear the drone of nectar-laden bees.

Use 1/8"-wide paper unless another width is specified. Before making the straight huskings called for in this design, refer to the instructions and diagrams on page 30. Then make a straight huskings form, using four pins only. Pins 1 and 2 should be 1/4" apart; Pins 2 and 3, and 3 and 4 are 1/8" apart.

Double Husking Flower
Using narrow peach paper, make twenty-four three-loop huskings for the petals.
Glue twelve petals together to make the upper layer and twelve petals together to make the lower layer.
Shape the upper layer by holding it in your palm and pressing gently at its center.
Glue the upper layer to the lower layer.
With a 6" length of narrow brick paper, make an inverted grape roll for the flower's center; glue the roll in place.

Single Husking Flowers (make four)
With narrow pale peach paper, make twelve petals, using only Pins 1, 2, and 3.

Glue these together, and shape them just as you shaped the upper layer of the double flower.
For the flower's center, add an inverted grape roll made with a 4" length of narrow brick paper.

Teardrop Flowers (make eight)
Glue together five brick 4" teardrops.
Add a soft ivory 2" loose circle for the flower's center.

Coral Bells (make fourteen bells)
To form a bell shape, roll a 2" length of coral paper, at an angle, on the needle tool.
Spread glue inside the bell so that it will retain its shape.
Glue the bells together to make three flower clusters, two with four bells each and one with six bells.

Heart Sprays (make five with two hearts each and one with three hearts)
Roll six cadet blue 2" open hearts and seven cadet blue 3" open hearts.
Curve six lengths of celedon green paper for the stems.
Glue two hearts to each of five stems, and three hearts to the last stem, placing the smaller hearts at each stem's end.

Spirals
Cut several lengths of celedon green paper, and using the needle tool, roll spirals at their ends.

Cut-Out Leaves (make twelve)
Cut a leaf from 3/8"-wide celedon green paper.
Crease it lightly and then fringe it.
Add short stems of celedon green paper to four of the leaves.

Scrolls
Roll four celedon green 2" loose scrolls.

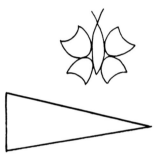

Butterfly
Cut the body from 5/8"-wide brown paper, using the pattern provided.
Roll the paper on a needle tool, beginning with the wide end; glue the pointed end down.
Add two yellow 6" bunny ears and two yellow 4" bunny ears as wings.
To make antennae, fold a 5/8" length of narrow yellow paper into a V, and glue it to the butterfly's body.

• Assembly

Arrange the flowers on an 8" x 10" pale green background, and glue them in place.

Add lengths of celedon green paper for the stems.

Add the leaves, spirals, and scrolls.

Position and glue the butterfly to the background.

Transfer the butterfly mat pattern to an 8" x 10" sheet of ivory sculpture paper, positioning it so that its bottom edge is 1" from the bottom of the paper and its sides are equidistant from the paper's edges.

Cut the butterfly shape out to make a butterfly-shaped mat.

Cut four lengths of 1/8" x 1/4" balsa, two 10" long and two 7-1/2" long.

Glue the balsa to the outer edges of the mat's back.

Roll approximately fourteen 1/8"-wide pegs, and glue them to the mat's back, 1/4" from the inside of the cut edge.

Place a small drop of glue onto the other end of each peg, and then place the pegged mat onto the background. The balsa and pegs should hold the mat 1/8" above the background.

Butterfly mat pattern

Cherry Blossoms

The time to quill these gorgeous cherry blossoms is during the winter. That's right. When your mood starts to drop with the temperature, lift your spirits by working on these lovely reminders of spring.

Use 1/8"-wide paper unless another width is specified.

Limb
Roll brown 4", 5", and 6" irregular squares and rectangles. These shapes should give the limb a rough appearance. The larger sizes are used on the thicker parts of the limb.

Also roll some 3" marquises.

Large Flowers (make four)
To make the flower's center, first glue a yellow 3" length of paper to a gold 1-1/4" length, end to end.

Fringe this 4-1/4" length, and then roll it into a fringed flower, beginning with the yellow end.

Fringe a 3/4" length of yellow 3/8"-wide paper, and glue it around the fringed flower.

For each of the five petals, roll nine 4" marquises, using narrow pink paper.

Glue these shapes together, curving each petal slightly.

Glue the five petals to the flower's center, overlapping each one as shown in the pattern.

Small Flowers (make five)
To make the center, first glue a yellow 2" length of paper to a gold 1" length, end to end.

Fringe and roll this 3" length into a fringed flower, beginning with the yellow end.

Fringe a 5/8" length of yellow 3/8"-wide paper, and glue it around the fringed flower.

For each of the five petals, roll five 3" marquises, using narrow deep rose paper.

Glue these shapes together, curving each petal slightly.

Glue the five petals to the center, overlapping each as shown in the pattern.

Buds (make five)
Using narrow deep rose paper, roll a 6" teardrop.

To make the calyx, cut narrow, pointed slivers of green paper, curl each one, and glue the slivers to the teardrop.

Using narrow green paper, roll a 4" grape roll, and glue it to the teardrop.

Large Leaves (make four to six)
Using narrow green paper, shape and then glue together six 3" marquises.

Small Leaves (make approximately fifty)
Using narrow green paper, make and glue together three 3" marquises.

• Assembly

Arrange the limb pieces on the background.

Then position the flowers, adjusting the limb pieces as necessary.

Glue the limb to the background and the flowers to the limb.

Position the buds and leaves, and glue them in place.

Christmas Tree and Wreath Designs

Mount these projects on lids, turn them into ornaments, or affix them to handmade gift tags. Classic Christmas shapes never lose their seasonal appeal.

Use 1/8"-wide paper unless another width is specified.

Christmas Tree

Tree
Using the pattern, make the tree with green 3" marquises, S scrolls, C scrolls, V scrolls, and open hearts.

Roll a C scroll using a 2" length of red 1/4"-wide paper.

Open the C scroll just enough to fit it over the trunk, and glue it in place.

Swags and Ornaments
Roll seven red 3" tight circles for ornaments.

To make swags for the tree, roll spirals with lengths of white paper.

• Assembly
Mount the tree on the lid.

Position the swags and ornaments, and glue them in place.

Wreath

Lower Layer
Roll sixteen green 3" open hearts and sixteen green 2" marquises.

Glue a marquise into each open heart.

Roll sixteen green 2" C scrolls.

Using the lower layer pattern, glue all these shapes together.

Upper Layer
Roll eight green 2" marquises and eight green 2" loose circles.

Glue these onto the lower wreath layer, using the illustration that shows a section of the assembled layers.

Bow and Streamers
Glue the ends of a 4" length of 1/4"-wide red paper back onto its center.

Center and glue a 4" length of white 1/8"-wide paper onto the red bow. (Curving the red paper before adding the white strip will make the bow smoother.)

For each streamer, glue a length of 1/8"-wide white paper down the center of a length of 1/4"-wide red paper.

Snip a V into the end of each streamer, and curl that end slightly.

Bells
Using two 24" lengths of red paper, roll two very conical grape rolls.

Make the clappers by adding a black 2" tight circle to each bell.

Leaves and Berries
Using narrow paper, roll three green 6" holly leaves and one red 3" tight circle.

• Assembly
Mount the layered wreath shape first.

Then, using the photo as a guide, glue the streamers, bow, bells, leaves, and berries to it.

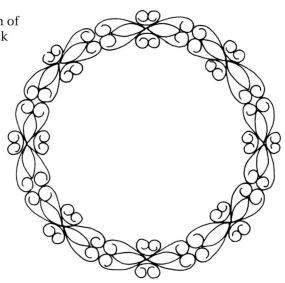

Section of assembled layers

Christmas Sampler

If you store it carefully, this sampler will last for years. And no matter how many times it appears, the project is likely to be a family favorite.

Use narrow paper unless another width is specified. Note that the individual designs should be mounted after they've been assembled.

Sampler Board

Paint a 9" x 7" sampler board white, and let it dry.

Lightly draw the following vertical lines on the board: a 5"-long line down from the top, 2-1/4" from the left side; a 3"-long line down from the top, 2-1/4" from the right side; and a 4"-long line up from the bottom edge, 4" from the right side.

Using the photo as a guide, draw three horizontal lines to create two squares (in the upper left and lower right corners) and five rectangles.

Glue 1/8"-wide red paper over all the pencil lines.

Glue strips of 1/4"-wide red paper around the sampler board's outside edges and around the heart cut-out's inside edges.

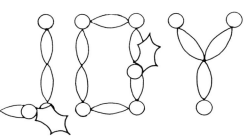

Joy

With 1/8"-wide paper, roll twelve green 2" marquises and ten green 2" tight circles.

Following the pattern, glue these shapes together to form the letters.

Then make five green 4" and three green 6" holly leaves. Roll five red 3" tight circles for berries.

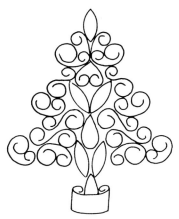

Tree

Using 1/8"-wide paper, make the tree with green 3" marquises, teardrops, open hearts, V scrolls, C scrolls, and S scrolls.

Roll eight red 3" tight circles, and glue them to the tree as trim.

Using 1/4"-wide paper, roll a red 2" C scroll.

Open the C scroll just enough to fit it over the trunk, and glue the scroll in place.

Poinsettia with Holly Leaves

To make the petals, roll twelve red 3-1/2" shaped marquises.

Glue six of the petals together to make the flower's lower layer and six to make the upper layer. (The petals in the upper layer should be glued at an angle so that their outer points are slightly raised.)

Roll several yellow 1/2" loose scrolls for the flower's center.

Glue these scrolls to the flower's upper layer.

Make three green 6" holly leaves.

Candles

Make nine green 6" holly leaves.

Roll three red 3" tight circles for berries.

Cut one 1-3/8" x 8" rectangle and two 1-1/8" x 8" rectangles from gold quill trim.

On the needle quilling tool, roll each rectangle lengthwise, and glue it closed to make a candle.

Roll three yellow 3" teardrops to make flames.

Bells

Make the two bells by rolling two red 24" pointed grape rolls from 1/8"-wide paper.

Make clappers by adding a black 2" tight circle to each bell.

Roll six green 6" holly leaves and two red 3" tight circles for berries.

Wreath

To make the lower layer, roll sixteen green 3" open hearts and sixteen green 2" marquises, using 1/8"-wide paper.

Next, glue a marquise into each open heart.

Also with 1/8"-wide paper, roll sixteen green 2" C scrolls.

Glue the shapes together, following the lower layer pattern.

To make the upper layer, use 1/8"-wide paper to make eight green 2" marquises and eight green 2" loose circles.

Glue these to the lower layer, as shown in the sectional pattern of the assembled layers.

Make a bow shape by gluing both ends of a 4" length of 1/4"-wide red paper back into the length's center.

Center and glue a 4" length of 1/8"-wide white paper along the length of the red paper. (Curving the first strip before adding the second will make the bow smoother.)

To create the streamers, curve two lengths of 1/4"-wide red paper slightly, glue 1/8"-wide white strips down their centers, and snip a V into the end of each streamer.

Make five green 6" holly leaves and two red 3" tight circles for berries.

Section of assembled layers

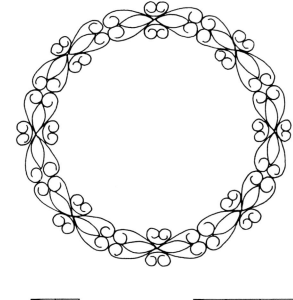

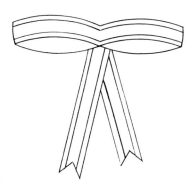

Packages

The packages (left to right) are all made with 1/8"-wide paper and are shaped as follows: four sky blue 4" squares; four white 3" squares; nine gold 4" squares; six red 4" rectangles; sixteen deep blue 4" squares; six sky blue 4" rectangles; and four red 4" squares.

Using the photo as a guide, choose contrasting colors of narrow paper for the ribbons and bows.

Position the sky blue, gold, deep blue, and red packages to make the lower layer; make the upper layer by gluing the white, red, and sky blue packages on top of them.

Medallion Ornaments

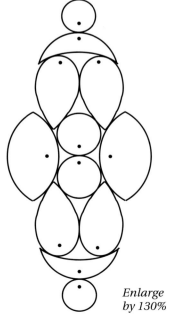

*Enlarge
by 130%*

These medallion shapes make pretty seasonal ornaments, of course, but they look just as attractive suspended year-round from a ceiling or doorway and can even be used to embellish a box. The eccentric shapes are especially beautiful when light and shade accentuate their graceful arcs and curves.

Use 1/8"-wide paper for the entire design. The instructions will yield one ornament.

• **Shapes and Assembly**
Note that the shapes described are all eccentric. Roll two bright white 18" fans, four bright white 15" teardrops, two bright white 6" circles, two crimson 9" circles, and two crimson 15" crescents. Using the pattern, position and glue these shapes together.

Diamond Star

Carpenter Wheel

Quilt-Block Ornaments

The geometric shapes in these colorful ornaments are more likely to be uniform in size if you make them on a quilling designer/board. Let your loose circles expand in the third largest mold (not the second), and then pinch them into squares and diamonds. Experiment, by all means, with other color combinations.

Enlarge each pattern by 144%

Use 6" lengths of 1/4"-wide paper for all elements of both designs.

Color Guide for Patterns
A = crimson
B = holiday green
C = bright white

Diamond Star

Using the pattern and the color guide, make eight squares and thirty-two diamonds.

Beginning with the center shapes and using the pattern, assemble the star's shapes and glue them together.

Carpenter Wheel

Make thirty-two diamonds and eight squares, once again using the pattern and color guide.
Assemble and glue the wheel's shapes.

64

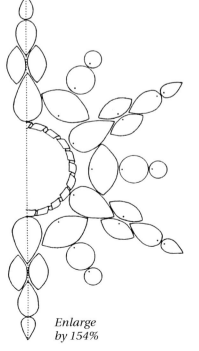

*Enlarge
by 154%*

Baby's First Christmas

Celebrate baby's first Christmas with this personalized tree ornament. Its eccentric shapes radiate from the center medallion in a joyful burst of pure white.

Use bright white 1/8"-wide paper for the entire design.

• **Shapes and Assembly**

Cut two 1-3/8" circles from white sculpture paper, and set one circle aside.

Position the other circle on your quilling board.

Make a spiral, and glue it around the circle's circumference.

Roll the following eccentric shapes: six 9" teardrops, six 9" fans, twelve 6" fans, six 6" loose circles, six 6" teardrops, six 3" teardrops, and six 3" loose circles.

Using the pattern as a guide, glue these shapes together around the spiral.

On the second circle, print the baby's name and the year.

Glue this circle to the ornament's front.

Twisted-Loop Ornaments

Whether you hang them on your Christmas tree or incorporate them into a seasonal centerpiece, you'll find that these brightly colored floral projects are both attractive and easy to make.

Use crimson paper for all parts of both designs.

Ornament Number One

Using 2-1/4" lengths of 3/8"-wide paper, make thirty twisted loops.

With 1/8"-wide paper, roll one 6" grape roll and twelve 3" grape rolls.

Beginning with the shapes in the center, glue the pieces together.

Ornament Number Two

Using 2-1/4" lengths of 3/8"-wide paper, make thirty twisted loops.

With 1/8"-wide paper, roll one 24" grape roll and eighteen 3" grape rolls.

Beginning with the shapes in the center, glue all the pieces together.

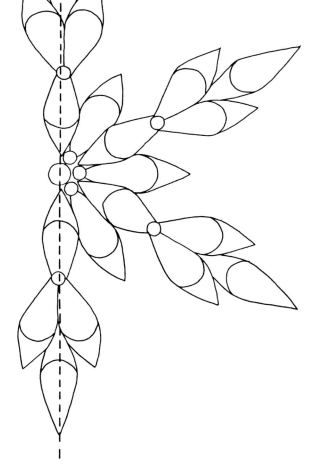

Christmas Gift Tags

The only disadvantage to these marvelous quilled tags is that they may command more attention than the gifts they embellish. If you're willing to take that risk, however, you'll find that they add a truly distinctive touch to any present.

When you make the ribbons and bows, use red 1/4"-wide paper in the designs that include silver quill trim and green paper of the same width in designs that include gold quill trim. The quantities specified in these instructions will yield one bell design and one candle design.

Ribbons and Streamers (make four of each)

Make a ribbon by gluing 1/8-wide" quill trim down the center of a 3" length of 1/4"-wide paper.

To make a streamer, first create a slight curve in a short length of 1/4"-wide paper.

Then glue quill trim down the streamer's center.

Snip a V into the streamer's end.

Bows (make two)

Form a bow by gluing the ends of a strip of 1/4"-wide paper back onto the strip's center.

Glue 1/8"-wide quill trim down the center of the strip. (Shaping the 1/4"-wide strip before adding the quill trim will make the bow smoother.)

Candles

Cut one 6" x 1-1/4" rectangle from quill trim.

Use a needle tool to roll the rectangle into a tight roll, and glue it closed.

Repeat with two 6" x 1" rectangles.

Using narrow yellow paper, make three 3" teardrops, and add one to each candle as a flame.

Bells and Clappers (make two of each)

Glue three 24" lengths of 1/8"-wide quill trim together, end to end. Using this 72" length, roll a very conical grape roll.

To shape the clapper, roll a tight circle from a 3" length of narrow black paper. Attach the clapper to the bell with a short length of narrow black paper.

Leaves and Berries

With narrow green paper, roll sixteen 5" holly leaves (eight for each tag).

To make berries, roll six 3" tight circles with 1/8"-wide red paper.

• Assembly

Cut two 3" x 6" rectangles from white accessory paper, and fold each one in half.

Glue the ribbons, streamers, and bows to these tags.

Glue the bells or candles in place.

Add eight holly leaves and three berries to each tag.

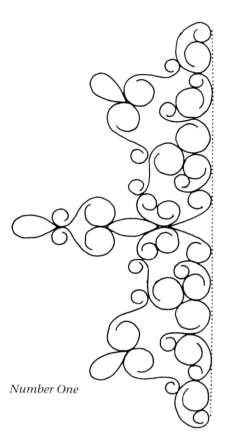

Number One

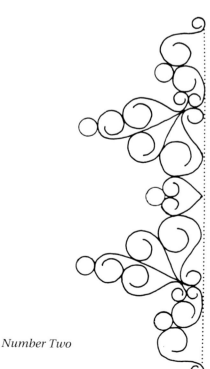

Number Two

3-D Ornaments

Three-dimensional ornaments are much easier to construct than you might think. Each pattern represents one-quarter of a completed design, so all you need to do is repeat each pattern four times and glue the four parts to a central post.

Use 1/8"-wide crimson paper and 1/8"-wide silver quill trim to make these two designs.

Ornament Number One (make four)

Roll one 4" V scroll, eight 4" C scrolls, one 4" marquise, ten 4" S scrolls, and three 4" teardrops.

Wrap a length of silver around each teardrop.

Position the shapes as shown in the pattern, and glue them together.

Ornament Number Two (make four)

Roll two 5" S scrolls, four 4" S scrolls, two 4" C scrolls, one 4" open heart, four 4" loose scrolls, and five 4" tight circles.

Wrap a length of silver around each tight circle.

Position the shapes as shown in the pattern, and glue them together.

• Assembly

Cut a 3-1/2" length of 1/8"-square balsa to make the post for Ornament Number One, and cut a 4-1/4" length for Ornament Number Two.

Paint each post red.

After the paint has dried, glue one quilled design to each of the posts' sides.

Add an extra 4" teardrop wrapped in silver to the ends of each ornament.

Snowflake Ornaments
and Gift Tags

What would Christmas be without snowflakes? Whether you use them to decorate your tree or to embellish a handmade card, these designs are bound to bring a bit of Christmas cheer into the lives of your loved ones.

Use bright white 1/8"-wide paper for these designs.

Ornament Number One

Roll eighteen 4" marquises, twelve 4" open hearts, twelve 4" teardrops, twelve 4" S scrolls, and six 2" loose circles.

Ornament Number Two

Roll six 4" marquises, six 4" open hearts, six 4" C scrolls, twelve 4" teardrops, twelve 4" open hearts, and twelve 4" S scrolls.

Gift Tag Number One

Roll twelve 2-1/2" teardrops and twelve 2-1/2" S scrolls.

Gift Tag Number Two

Roll six 2-1/2" marquises, six 2-1/2" open hearts, six 2-1/2" C scrolls, and six 2-1/2" teardrops.

• Assembly

To assemble these designs, position and glue the shapes together, beginning in the center and working out towards the points. (Note that classic snowflakes and other radial designs are easiest to assemble on a grid like the one pictured on page 17.)

To make cards or tags, simply glue the snowflake to a folded piece of colored card stock or heavy paper.

Ornament Number One

Gift Tag Number One

Gift Tag Number Two

Ornament Number Two

Santa Claus

Add a lighthearted touch to your Christmas tree with this whimsical Santa. His personalized list is bound to impress the children in your household.

Use 1/8"-wide paper unless another width is specified.

Head (Lower Layer)

Hat and Pompom
Fill in the hat outline with red 3" marquises.

Roll a bright white 18" grape roll, and glue it to the hat's peak.

Then roll loose scrolls, using 1/2" lengths of bright white narrow paper. Glue these scrolls to the grape roll.

Face and Beard
Fill in the outline of the face with flesh 3" marquises.

Roll a red 3" tight circle for the mouth.

Fill in the outline of the beard with bright white 3" loose circles.

Head (Upper Layer)

Hat Trim
Cut the hat trim pattern from bright white 5/8"-wide paper.

Using 1/2" lengths of bright white narrow paper, roll loose scrolls.

Glue these scrolls to the trim band, and glue the band in place.

Eyes, Nose, and Mustache
Roll two black 4" tight circles for eyes.

Roll a bright white 3" tight circle for the nose.

For each side of the mustache, glue together three bright white teardrops: 3", 4", and 5".

Glue all these features in place.

Body (Lower Layer)

Suit, Sleeves, Gloves, and Boots
Fill in the outlines for the suit and sleeves with red 3" marquises.

Fill in the outlines for the gloves and boots with black 3" marquises.

Body (Upper Layer)

Trim

Cut the fur trim patterns for the sleeves, suit, and boots from white 5/8"-wide paper.

Roll loose scrolls, using 1/2" lengths of bright white narrow paper, and glue them to the bands of paper.

Glue the bands in place.

Santa's List

Cut a 1-1/8" x 4-1/2" rectangle from white sculpture paper.

Print names on the rectangle; then roll its ends.

• Assembly

Glue the head to the body so that the beard overlaps the coat.

Glue the sleeves to the suit, with the beard overlapping the sleeves' tops.

Position Santa's list between the gloves, and glue it in place.

Sleeve trim

Boot trim

Suit trim

Elves

Handmade ornaments lend a personal touch to any Christmas tree, and these sets of elves are no exception. Make one or two each year; before long, you'll have an entire collection.

Use 1/8"-wide paper unless another width is specified. To make the second of the two elves described in each set, use the colors specified in parentheses.

Elves One and Two

Head and Hat

First, glue three 24" lengths of flesh paper together, end to end.

Then, using this 72" length, roll a rounded grape roll to serve as the elf's head.

Make ears with 3" lengths of flesh paper; shape them as shown in the pattern, and glue them in place.

Make the hair by gluing short, fringed lengths of narrow brown paper to the head.

With acrylics, paint features on the face.

Fill in the hat outline with holiday green (or red) 2" marquises.

Add five white 3" fringed flowers as a hat band.

Add a white 5" fringed flower to make the pompom.

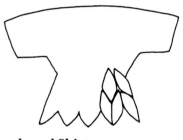

Hands and Shirt

Glue a flesh 1" teardrop to a flesh 4" teardrop to make each hand.

Fill in the shirt outline with holiday green (or red) 2" marquises and triangles.

Glue a length of gold (or black) paper around the waist to make a belt. Add a black (or gold) 4" square made with narrow paper as a buckle.

Collar and Scarf

Glue a loop of red (or white) paper at the top of the shirt as a collar.

Cut two lengths of red (or white) paper, notch one end of each, and add them to make the scarf lengths.

Add a small square of red (or white) paper to make a knot for the scarf.

Pants and Boots

Fill in the outline for the pants with red (or holiday green) 2" marquises.

Glue together five black 2" marquises and one black 2" crescent for each boot.

• Assembly

Glue the hat to the head and the head to the collar-and-scarf assembly. Onto the backs of the sleeves, glue the pointed ends of the teardrops that form the hands.

Glue the shirt over the top edge of the pants, and glue the boots in place by overlapping them slightly on top of the pants.

Elves Three and Four

Head and Hands

Follow the instructions for Elves
One and Two.

Hat

Fill in the outline with holiday
green (or red) 2" marquises.
Add a hat band made with a
length of red (or holiday
green) paper.
Make and attach a white 5"
fringed flower pompom.

Shirt

Fill in the outline with red (or
holiday green) 2" marquises
and triangles.
Glue a length of white paper at
the bottom of the shirt.

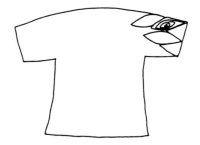

Fold a length of white paper into a V, and glue it to the shirt as a collar.

Using narrow paper, roll white 1/2" loose scrolls.

Spread glue on the collar and on the shirt strip; then sprinkle the loose scrolls on both.

Add two white 3" tight circles made with narrow paper for buttons.

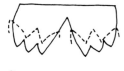

Pants and Boots

Fill in the outline for the pants with red (or holiday green) 2" marquises and triangles.

Glue together five black 2" marquises and one black 2" crescent for each boot.

• Assembly

Glue the hat to the head and the head to the shirt.

Glue the shirt so that it overlaps the pointed ends of the teardrops that form the hands.

Glue the shirt and pants together.

Glue the pants and boots together so that the boots overlap the pants.

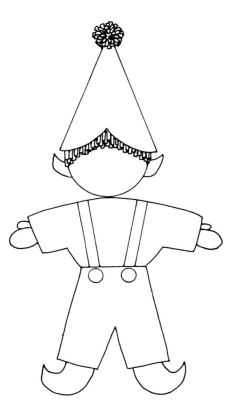

Elves Five and Six

Head and Hands

Follow the instructions for Elves One and Two.

Hat

Fill in the outline with red (or holiday green) 2" marquises.

Add a white 5" fringed flower pompom.

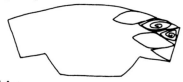

Shirt

Fill in the outline with white 2" marquises and triangles.

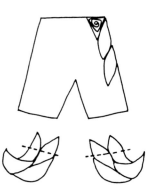

Pants, Suspenders, and Boots

Fill in the outline of the pants with holiday green (or red) 2" marquises and triangles, and attach the pants to the shirt. (You may overlap the pants on the shirt; the suspenders will stand away from the shirt front if you do.)

To make suspenders, glue two lengths of red (or holiday green) paper from the top of the pants to the shoulders.

Make buttons by adding two white 3" tight circles made with narrow paper to the pants.

Glue together three black 2" marquises and one black 1" crescent to make each boot.

• Assembly

Glue the hat to the head and the head to the shirt.

Glue the hands to the shirt so that the shirt overlaps their pointed ends.

Glue the pants to the boots, with the pants overlapping the boots slightly.

Shamrock Bouquet

Celebrate St. Patrick's day by offering this delicate bouquet of shamrocks to someone you love. Who knows? It just might bring luck to both of you.

Shamrocks (make ten)
Glue together three holiday green
   4" open hearts.
Add a length of holiday green
   paper as a stem.

• Assembly
Glue five shamrocks to the
   background.

Arrange and glue the other five,
   layering them as shown in the
   photograph.
Gather the stems in their centers,
   and glue them together.
Add a small, green bow.

Halloween Decoration

Quill a ghoulish gathering for a Halloween decoration. This whimsical design will add that special, haunting touch to your fall decorations.

Use 1/8"-wide paper unless another width is specified. The background consists of a 6" x 6" square of orange mat board.

Jack-o'-Lantern
Fill in this pattern with orange 3" marquises, shaping the outer marquises slightly to create an even outline.

Add a green 3" teardrop for the stem.

Roll three black 2" triangles for the eyes and nose and a black 2" crescent for the mouth.

Bats (make two)
Cut the bat pattern from black paper.

Curve the tips of the wings.

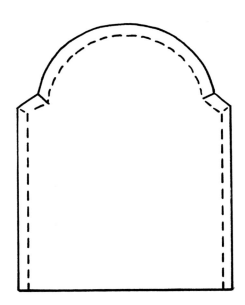

Tombstone
Using the pattern, first cut out the exterior shape from ivory sculpture paper.

Print R I P (rest in peace) on the tombstone.

Score the tombstone on the dotted lines, and slice through the two short solid lines at each end of the arched top section.

Then fold back the scored edges slightly.

Ghost
Fill in the ghost pattern with white 3" S scrolls.

Outline the entire ghost by gluing a length of grey paper around it.

To make the eyes, cut two small black ovals.

To make the mouth, cut two lengths of black paper, one slightly shorter than the other. Curve both lengths, and glue them together.

• Assembly
Glue the tombstone to the background.

Position the jack-o'-lantern, ghost, and bats, and glue them in place, overlapping the ghost and jack-o'-lantern over the tombstone.

If necessary, use pegs behind the shapes to keep them parallel to the background.

Valentine Hang-Up

No potential sweetheart could possibly resist this quilled valentine. Be forewarned, though; you may be called fickle if you give away as many of these love tokens as you'd like.

Use narrow paper unless another width is specified.

Heart
Using the pattern provided, cut a heart from lightweight cardboard.

Then cut a piece of red fabric that is slightly larger than the heart.

Glue the fabric to the cardboard, turning the fabric's edges under and gluing them to the cardboard's back.

Glue white, gathered lace around the heart.

Then glue a 1/8"-wide, red ribbon loop to the top center of the heart's back.

To make a backing, cut another heart, and glue it onto the back.

Border
Roll seventeen white 3" marquises, seventeen white 3" open hearts, eleven white 4" tight circles, and one 4" V scroll.

Glue one marquise inside each open heart.

Position the pieces, using the pattern as a guide, and then glue them to the fabric heart.

Flower
Glue together five white 3" teardrops; make the flower's center by adding a red jewel.

Bud
Roll a white 1-1/2" teardrop for the bud.

Tear a short length of green paper for a stem.

Cut a slot in one end of this length, spread the two sections apart, and cut a point on each one.

Glue the teardrop between the spread sections.

Scrolls and Leaves
Roll one green 2" loose scroll and two green 1-1/2" loose scrolls.

Cut two leaves from 3/8"-wide soft green paper.

Using scissors, fringe their edges, and curl each leaf slightly.

• Assembly
Glue the two leaves to the flower.

Position the flower in the fabric heart's center, and glue it in place.

Add the bud and the three loose scrolls.

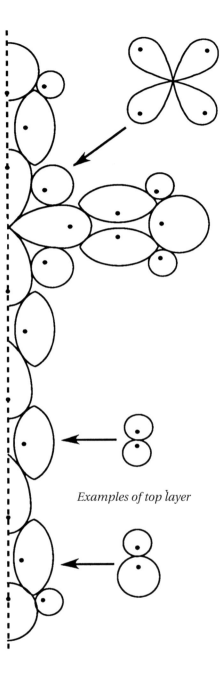

Examples of top layer

80

Use 1/8"-wide bright white paper for the entire design, and remember that every shape is eccentric.

Lower Layer

Roll six 9" teardrops, twelve 9" fans, four 9" loose circles, four 6" loose circles, and eight 3" loose circles.

Beginning with the four teardrops at the center, glue all these shapes together.

Upper Layer

Roll four 6" teardrops, four 6" loose circles, and eight 3" loose circles.

Glue together the points of the four teardrops; then glue the assembled pieces to the center of the cross.

Glue four pairs of 6" and 3" loose circles together; add these over the fans near each point of the cross.

Glue two pairs of 3" loose circles together, and add these over the fans on the lower arm of the cross.

Cross

This simple cross design can be displayed year-round, but it's especially suitable for the Easter season. Its eccentric shapes and two layers are easily made and assembled.

Quilling on Lace Eggs

These delicately quilled lace eggs make wonderful Easter presents, though you may find it difficult to part with them once you've made them.

To make a lace egg, you'll need a styrofoam egg that measures approximately 3-1/2" x 2-1/2", lace (pure cotton only), some 1"-wide ruffled, decorative lace, a hot glue gun, lace stiffener, plastic wrap, and rust-proof pins. Select spring colors for the various shapes in the quilled designs. Use the photograph as an assembly guide, or arrange the designs in any way you choose. Use 1/8"-wide paper unless another width is specified. The instructions will yield one egg.

Lace Egg

Cut the styrofoam egg in half, lengthwise. Cut a 1"-diameter flat area on the bottom of one half, so that the finished lace egg won't roll.

Make two paper patterns by wrapping each half of the egg in paper; the patterns should completely cover the rounded portion of each half and should include a portion that will extend over the flat side of each half by about 1/2".

Using these paper patterns, cut two pieces of cotton lace to size.

Next, wrap each half of the egg in plastic wrap, securing the wrap with transparent tape.

Drench each piece of lace with fabric stiffener, and then wrap the egg halves with the lace, smoothing the lace over the rounded portions so that no wrinkles or bumps remain.

Use rust-proof pins to fasten the lace to the flat surface of each egg half. Insert the pins into the flat surfaces, as close to their edges as possible. (If you've cut the lace correctly, each piece should overlap the flat surface slightly.)

Trim any excess lace away from the waste side of the pins, leaving only a thin lip of lace on the flat section, just enough for the pins to hold.

Allow the lace to dry thoroughly (about twenty-four hours).

Then remove the pins, and carefully work the styrofoam halves away from the stiffened lace. This will take some patience, especially if you want to keep the styrofoam intact! Try not to damage the thin lace lip.

Now apply hot glue to the lace lips, and press the egg halves together.

Measure the distance around the egg (lengthwise); then cut two pieces of 1"-wide, ruffled, decorative lace, each slightly longer than the measured distance.

Sew the lace strips together, edge to edge, with the lacy edge on each one facing out.

Wrap the strip around the egg, covering its glued seam.

Overlap the strips' ends slightly, and glue them together.

To disguise the seam in the lace strip, wrap a piece of 1/4"-wide ribbon around it. Make sure that the ribbon's ends overlap at the back of the egg; you'll disguise that area with a punch flower when you assemble your project.

Curled Flowers, Made Using a Rectangle (make three)

For each petal, use a 1/2" length of 3/8"-wide paper.

To make the flower's center, roll a 5" loose circle with 1/4"-wide paper, and glue it in place.

Fringed Flowers (make three)

Use a 3" length of 1/4"-wide paper for each flower.

Punch Flowers (make three or four)

With a 1/4"-round paper punch, punch out five circles.

Place a dab of glue in the center of a tiny square of paper, and using tweezers, arrange the petals in the dot of glue, holding each one at an upward angle as you do.

Make the center by rolling a narrow 1" tight circle and gluing it in place.

Buds with Leaves (make eight or nine)

Roll and shape a 3" teardrop.

Cut a slot in the end of a short length of green paper, and curl the two slit sections back away from each other.

Glue the teardrop into this slot.

Slightly curl the other end of the green paper.

Add two green 2-1/2" teardrops for leaves.

Fringed Leaves (make six)

Cut a leaf shape from 3/8"-wide paper, and fringe both edges.

**Scrolls
(make several
of each type)**
Roll loose scrolls and
S scrolls, using 1",
1-1/2", and 2"
lengths of paper.

Butterfly
Glue together two 3"
teardrops to make
the body.

Add a 2" V scroll made with
narrow black paper.

Bow
Tie a small bow, using a piece
of 1/4"-wide satin ribbon.

• Assembly
Glue two fringed leaves to the
back of each curled flower.
Next, position the bow and the
curled flowers with leaves, and
glue them to the egg.

Glue the butterfly near one
curled flower.
Glue one or two loose scrolls to
each fringed flower, and then
glue these in place.
Add all but one of the punch
flowers and all the buds.
Fill in with several S scrolls; place
these wherever they look best.
Use the last punch flower to
cover the overlapped ends
of the ribbon.

Quilling on Satin Eggs

Encourage the Easter bunny to include a few of these charming satin eggs among those he hides on Easter day. They're everything but edible: delightfully colorful, surprisingly sturdy, and downright fun.

Use 1/8"-wide paper for all three designs unless another width is specified.

Bunny with Easter Basket Design

Bunny Body
Glue two white 24" lengths together, end to end.

Roll a white 48" tight circle with this glued length.

Bunny Head
Roll a white 24" tight circle.
To make whiskers, fringe a short length of narrow tan paper on each end.
Roll a 1" tight circle of narrow tan paper for the nose, and glue it to the whiskers.

Using narrow pink paper, roll two 1" tight circles for the eyes.
To make each ear, first glue a pink 2" length and a white 3" length together.
Then, beginning with the pink end, roll a teardrop.
Glue the body to the satin egg.
Then glue the eyes, ears, and the whiskers with nose to the head.
Glue the head to the body.

Bunny Arms and Feet
Roll two white 3" teardrops, and glue these in place as arms, with one extended at an angle so that it can hold the basket.
Roll two white 4" teardrops for feet, and glue each one to the body at a slight angle.

 Basket
Roll a pink 18" grape roll, and flatten the bottom slightly.
Add a short length of narrow pink paper for the handle.

Eggs
Using narrow paper in a variety of bright colors, roll eight 6" grape rolls.
Glue four of these eggs inside the basket with two at the top of the basket where they'll show. Set the remaining four eggs aside.
Glue the basket to the tilted arm.

 Tulips (make eight)
Roll a 2" bunny ear, using narrow yellow paper.
Cut two lengths of narrow green paper, and cut a point at one end of each.
Glue the lower halves of the lengths together to form a stem.
Curl the unglued, pointed ends of each stem away from each other, and glue the bunny-ear tulip into the V-shaped space between them.

Leaves (make seventeen)
Cut a leaf shape from green paper, and curl one end.

• Assembly
Glue two or three leaves to each flower.
Arrange four flower-and-leaf sets, with an egg at the base of each, on each side of the bunny; glue these in place.
Add the remaining four sets, two on each side of the bunny.

Flowers and Butterfly Design

Ribbon and Bow
Wrap a length of teal paper vertically around the egg, gluing it to the egg's top and bottom only.
Make two loops with 2-1/4" lengths of teal paper.
Cut two teal streamers, each approximately 1-1/4" long, and cut a notch in one end of each.
Glue the streamers and loops to the egg's top.
Roll two teal 4" teardrops and one teal 2" teardrop.
Glue these together, and then glue them to the loops.

Teardrop Flower
Glue together five deep rose 3" teardrops.
Add a small pearl to make the flower's center.

Bunny Ear Flowers (make three)
Glue together three pink 3" bunny ears.
To make the flower's center, add a 2" tight circle made with narrow raspberry paper.

Scrolls with Leaves (make two)
Roll a cadet blue 2" loose scroll.
To make the leaf, shape a cadet blue 2" teardrop, and glue it to the scroll.

| 1/2" | 3/4" | 1/2" |

Looped Leaves (make six)
Cut a 1-3/4" length of cadet blue paper.
Mark sections on this length, as shown in the diagram, at 1/2", 3/4", and 1/2".
Shape each section into a loop, and glue the loops together.

Butterfly
To make the body, roll a very slender 4" gold marquise.
The wings consist of two bright yellow 5" teardrops and two bright yellow 3" teardrops; glue these to the body.
Fold a short length of gold into a V, cut points on its ends, and glue it to the body to make antennae.

• Assembly
Position the teardrop flower on the egg, and glue it in place.
Add the two scrolls with teardrop leaves.
Glue two looped leaves to each bunny ear flower; then glue the assembled flowers to the egg.
Position and glue the butterfly.

Flower and Bird Design

Ribbon and Bow
Wrap a length of teal paper vertically around the egg, and glue it to the egg at the top and bottom only.
Make two loops with 2-1/4" lengths of teal paper.
Cut two teal streamers, each approximately 1-1/4" long, and cut a notch in one end of each.
Glue the streamers and loops to the top of the egg.
Roll two teal 4" teardrops and one teal 2" teardrop.
Glue these together, and then glue them to the loops.

Teardrop Flower
Glue together five purple 3" teardrops.
Add a small pearl to make the flower's center.

Bunny Ear Flowers (make three)
Glue together three lilac 3" bunny ears.
To make the flower's center, add a 2" tight circle made with narrow yellow paper.

Scrolls with Leaves (make two)
Roll a cadet blue 2" loose scroll.
To make the leaf, add a cadet blue 2" teardrop.

Looped Leaves (make six)
Cut a 1-3/4" length of cadet blue paper.
Mark sections along its length, as shown in the diagram, at 1/2", 3/4", and 1/2".
Shape each section into a loop, and then glue the loops together.

Bird
Roll a turquoise 4" half circle for the body.
Add a turquoise 2" loose circle for the head, and a small turquoise V for a beak.
Roll two turquoise 2-1/2" shaped teardrops for the wings, and glue them to the body.
Roll a turquoise 1-1/2" loose scroll and a turquoise 2" loose scroll.
First glue these together, and then glue them to the body to make a tail.

• Assembly
Glue the teardrop flower to the egg.
Add the two scrolls with teardrop leaves.
Glue two looped leaves to each bunny ear flower; then glue the flowers to the egg.
Glue the bird to the egg.

Border for a Wedding Announcement

To make an elegant wedding gift, one that the happy couple will treasure for years to come, first mount the printed announcement, and then surround it with an elegant quilled border. This design emphasizes fringed flowers and flowers made with eccentric shapes.

Use 1/8"-wide paper unless another width is specified.

Double Teardrop Flower

Roll and shape ten bright white 9" eccentric teardrops.

Construct the lower layer by gluing five of the teardrops together.

Glue another five together to make the upper layer.

Glue the upper layer to the lower layer.

Glue a 5" length of yellow paper to a 3/4" length of gold quill trim, end to end.

Repeat to make two more duo-tone strips.

From these strips, roll three tight circles; roll each from its yellow end.

Attach these circles to the upper layer to make a center for the flower.

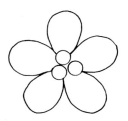

Medium Teardrop Flowers (make three)

Glue together five bright white 6" eccentric teardrops.

The flower's center is made with three tight circles. Construct these just as you did when you made the circles for the double teardrop flower, but use a 3-1/2" length of yellow paper and a 1/2" length of gold quill trim for each strip.

Small Teardrop Flowers (make six)

Glue together five bright white 3" eccentric teardrops.

Make three tight circles for the flower's center, following the instructions for the double teardrop center, but use a 1-1/2" length of yellow paper and a 1/2" length of gold quill trim to make each strip.

Fringed Flowers (make six)

Roll a 4" length of 3/8"-wide bright white fringed paper into a tight circle, and shape a fringed flower from it.

Bud Sprays (make four)

Curve a green 1" strip slightly.

Roll three green tight circles: a 1", a 1-1/2", and a 2".

Glue the circles to the green strip, placing the smallest tight circle at the strip's end.

Quilled Leaves on Stems

Roll thirty-six green 3" marquises.

Glue these to short lengths of curved green paper.

Looped Leaves (make four)

Cut a green 4-3/4" strip.

Mark sections, as shown in the illustration, at 3/4", 1", 1-1/4", 1", and 3/4".

Shape each section into a loop, and glue the loops together to form looped leaves.

• Assembly

Mount the wedding invitation slightly below the center of an 8" x 10" mat.

Position and glue the flowers and greenery, using the pattern as a guide. Begin with the center flowers at the top and bottom, and work outward toward the border's sides.

| 3/4" | 1" | 1-1/4" | 1" | 3/4" |

Looped leaf sections

Mr. and Mrs. William Paul Ryan
request the honour of your presence
at the marriage of their daughter
Janet Lynn
to
Mr. John Thomas Clark
on Saturday, the second of June
at seven o'clock in the evening
Brookside Presbyterian Church
Columbus, Ohio

Calla Lily Border Design

Quilled borders are as varied as their makers. In this stunning design, originally created for a wedding announcement, simplicity and elegance walk hand-in-hand. The delicacy of the two fern-and-flower clusters is accentuated by a plain black background.

Use 1/8"-wide paper unless another width is specified.

Calla Lilies (make six)

Fold 1/2"-wide white quilling paper in half lengthwise.

Cut the calla lily shape while the paper is folded, making one end rounded and the other pointed.

Open the paper shape, and curl its pointed end back over the quilling tool or your finger.

Using tweezers, put a drop of glue on the rounded bottom end of the flower, and pinch that end closed. Allow the glue to dry.

To make the lily's center, roll a fringed flower from a 1/4"-wide, 1/2"- to 3/4"-long strip of pale pink paper. Do not spread the fringes out.

Glue the rolled flower into the center of the lily.

Add a length of celedon green paper for a stem; you may cut an angle on the flower end of this stem if you wish.

Punch Flowers (make eight)

Punch out four tiny white circles, using a 1/8"-round paper punch.

Place a dab of glue in the center of a tiny square of paper.

Stand the petals on edge in the glue, and pinch them in place with a pair of tweezers. Overlap the petals slightly.

To make the flower's center, roll a tight circle with a 1/2" length of narrow pale pink paper.

Scrolls (make five)

Roll a short length of celedon green paper into a loose scroll.

 Fringed Flowers (make nine)

Roll a fringed flower, using a 1-1/2" length of 1/4"-wide white paper.

Ferns (make four)

Roll six to seven celedon green 1-1/2" tight circles, and set them aside.

Cut a length of celedon green paper as a stem.

Lilies of the Valley (make four)

Roll three pale pink 1-1/2" bunny ears.

Glue them to the underside of a slightly curved length of celedon green paper.

Bow

Using a 5" length of pale pink paper, shape a simple bow by forming two loops in the center of the length.

• Assembly

As you follow these instructions, use the photo as a placement guide.

Glue two scrolls to each of two calla lily stems, and one scroll to a fern stem.

Position the calla lilies and their stems on the mat, and glue them in place.

Glue a stem in place for each fern.

Arrange and glue sets of six or seven tight circles near but not touching each fern stem.

Glue the lilies of the valley in place.

Next, add a cluster of four punch flowers to each grouping.

Position and glue the bow in the upper grouping.

Add a cluster of four fringed flowers to the upper grouping, allowing one to overlap the bow just slightly.

Add the five remaining fringed flowers to the lower grouping.

Cut-paper leaves

Mr. and Mrs. Philip Leinwand
and
Mr. and Mrs. Harry Friedman
request the honor of your presence
at the marriage of their children
Marina Rose
and
Eric Zev
on Sunday, September 16
nineteen hundred and seventy-nine
at twelve o'clock noon
664 Thwaites Place
Napanoch, New York

Bridal Canopy
Border Design

Inspired by the chuppah *(or bridal canopy) under which Jewish couples are married, this design, with its elegant scrolls, beaded flowers, and lily of the valley sprays, is suitable for wedding invitations of all faiths.*

Use ivory quilling paper for the entire design. You'll need an 8" x 10" mat board, a craft knife, a hole punch, and nine beads (3 mm or less in diameter). Lace or beading may be used instead of paper to create the horizontal borders; 13" of either material, in a 1/8" width, will be required.

Cutting the Mat Board
The 4" x 5-1/4" mat opening is centered vertically in the 8" x 10" mat, with 2" on either side. It is located 2" from the bottom of the board and 2-3/4" from the top.

Columns with Flowering Vines
Using the pattern as a guide, position and glue two 6-1/4" lengths of 3/8"-wide paper to make the vertical columns.

At the base of each column, center and glue a 5/8" length of 1/8"-wide paper.

Below this short length, center and glue a 3/4" length of 3/8"-wide paper.

To make the two flowers for the columns, first use a hole punch to punch four circles from 3/8"-wide paper.

Curl each circle slightly; then overlap and glue them together as shown in the pattern.

Use a single bead as the center of each flower, or make centers by rolling 1-1/2" tight circles with narrow paper.

To make the four cut-paper leaves, first draw the leaf shapes onto 3/8"-wide paper, as shown in the illustration.

Then use a craft knife to cut out the inside opening of each leaf.

Finally, cut the leaves from the length of paper.

Using 1/8"-wide paper, make six 5" shaped marquises for the quilled leaves.

Working from the base of each column upward, make the scrolls by gluing lengths of 1/8"-wide paper on edge.

Position and glue the flowers, cut-paper leaves, and quilled leaves.

Canopy Design
To make the horizontal canopy borders, position and glue two 6-1/4" lengths of 1/8"-wide paper as shown in the pattern. The lower of these lengths should rest on top of the columns. (Note that these lengths may be embellished by crimping or pleating them or by cutting them from 3/8"-wide paper with scalloping or pinking shears. You may also substitute 1/8"-wide beading or lace if you prefer.)

To make the three large flowers, follow the instructions for making the small flowers, but include five petals in each flower instead of four, and carefully crimp each petal before assembling the flowers.

Make four small flowers and twelve cut-paper leaves, following the directions given previously.

Also make six 5" shaped marquises for the quilled leaves.

To make each of the four lily of the valley sprays, first roll two loose circles from 4" lengths of 1/8"-wide paper and one 3" loose circle from the same width paper, leaving a very short length of unglued paper on each circle to serve as a stem.

Then shape each circle into a bell.

Tear a 2"-long length of paper, and roll 1/2" at one end into a loose circle.

Glue the bells to this stem, with the smaller bell closest to the stem's rolled end.

Make several loose scrolls, using short lengths of paper.

Glue the flowers in place first, and then position and glue the lily of the valley sprays, scrolls, cut-paper leaves, and quilled leaves.

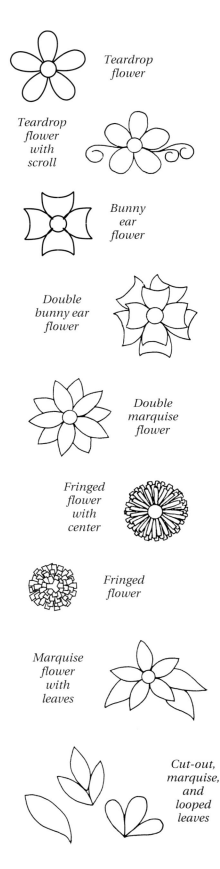

Teardrop flower

Teardrop flower with scroll

Bunny ear flower

Double bunny ear flower

Double marquise flower

Fringed flower with center

Fringed flower

Marquise flower with leaves

Cut-out, marquise, and looped leaves

Floral Gift Tags

Buying gift tags is certainly less time-consuming than quilling them, but there's nothing like a handmade tag to let someone special know how much you care. Choose colors and styles to complement your gift or its wrapping, and by all means create arrangements of your own.

Use narrow paper unless another width is specified. Patterns are provided for each flower type; use the photographs (or your own design concepts) to arrange the individual shapes.

Cards

To make the card, cut a rectangle and fold it in half.

Glue backgrounds for your flower designs onto each card; loops or lines of ribbon and lace will both look lovely.

• Shapes and Assembly

As you make the required shapes, take advantage of the following hints:

Use 3" lengths when you make the teardrops or bunny ears for small flowers.

Several of the larger flowers pictured are made with 5" lengths.

When layering shapes, incorporate larger shapes into the lower layer and smaller shapes into the upper layer.

To vary the flowers' centers, use small jewels or pearls for some and quilled tight circles for others.

Add fringed flowers, some with centers and others duo-tone.

Make quilled or cut-out leaves, and use small scrolls for greenery.

Gift Cards

Quilled cards make lovely accompaniments to presents. Purchase or make the tri-fold card blank, and quill a design to suit the occasion. The lucky recipient may want to frame your quilled creation.

Lily of the Valley Design

Use narrow paper for all parts of this design.

Stems (make three)
Roll a small scroll at one end of a length of soft green paper.

Buds (make three sets)
Roll three white 1-1/2" tight circles, and glue them to the scrolled end of the stem.

Flowers

Roll several bunny ears, using 2-1/2", 3", and 3-1/2" lengths of white paper.
Glue the bunny ears to the stems, placing the smallest ones closest to the stems' ends. (Position most of the bunny ears flat on either side of the stem, but glue a few to the stem at an angle.)

• Assembly
Arrange the three stems (with attached flowers) on the background, and glue them in place.
Roll several scrolls, using soft green paper, and add them to the background.
Make a bow with bright yellow paper, and glue it to the gathered stems.

Orange Flowers Design

Use narrow paper for all parts of this design. The petal shape in this design is a variation of the rolled heart. Its three points aren't really pointed; they're just slightly rounded.

Flowers (make three)
Roll six orange 8" rolled hearts for the petals, and glue them together.
To make the flower's center, add a brown inverted grape roll.

Stems and Leaves
To make stems, roll three brown spirals.
Roll six brown shaped marquises to serve as leaves: three 7", two 5", and one 4".

• Assembly
Arrange the stems on the background, and glue them in place.
Add the flowers.
Add the leaves, placing some flat on the background and others at an angle.

Swan Design

Both the tail and wing feathers are made using the loop method. To make these two-loop pieces, fold the paper length 1/4" off-center. Shape a loop with the shorter section, and then shape a loop with the longer section. Use 1/8"-wide paper for this entire design.

Body
First make five white tail feathers, using one 3-1/2", two 3", and two 2-1/2" lengths.
Glue these feathers together.
Fill in the rest of the body with white 3" marquises.
To make the beak, roll a black 3" shaped teardrop, and glue it in place.
Add a black 1" tight circle for the eye.

Wing
The wing consists of eight, two-loop feathers. The smallest is made with a 2-1/2" length. Each of the other seven is 1/8" longer than the one before; the longest is 3-3/8".
Curl the ends of these feathers slightly.
Glue them together to make the wing, and then glue the wing to the body.

Gift Bags

To transform even the humblest gift into one that's truly special, present it in a handmade, quilled bag. These decorative containers make lovely gifts themselves.

Use 1/8"-wide paper for the quilled designs unless another width is specified.

Bags (make three)

To make a bag, first cut the bag pattern out from white sculpture paper. (To cut a scalloped edge at the top of the bag, use wavy-blade scissors or a wave cutter.)

Score the paper on the dotted lines, and then fold along those lines.

Glue the shaded section inside the bag.

Overlap the end sections, and glue them together.

To make the handle, thread a ribbon through a small hole on either side of the bag.

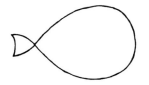

Balloon Design

Choose five bright colors, one for each balloon.

To make each balloon, roll a 24" length of paper, and let it expand in the largest mold on the quilling designer/board.

Shape the loose circle into an eccentric teardrop, making sure that all the interior points lie in a straight line.

Add a 3" bunny ear of the same color to each balloon.

Also make strings for four of the five balloons by adding lengths of black paper to them.

Make the lower layer by arranging four balloons on the bag, three with strings and one without.

Glue one balloon and string on top of that layer.

Gather the strings, cut them off evenly at their bottom ends, and glue them together.

Bouquet Design

To make each of the three flowers, glue together five teal 3" teardrops, and add a white 3" tight circle for the flower's center.

Add three green paper lengths for stems; these should be 1-3/4", 2", and 2-1/2" in length.

Cut two green lengths for leaves, one 3" and the other 2-3/4", and cut points on their ends. Curl the pointed ends slightly.

To make the scrolls, cut five lengths of green paper, and roll loose scrolls on one end of each.

Using the photo as a guide, arrange the flowers with stems, scrolls, and leaves, and glue them to the bag.

To make a small gift tag, cut a 2" x 1-3/4" piece of white sculpture paper, and fold it in half.

Make the flower by gluing together five teal 1-1/2" teardrops.

Add a white 1-1/2" tight circle for the flower's center.

Add one small green scroll.

Fringed Flowers Design

Roll three duo-tone fringed flowers, using a 2" length of 3/8"-wide raspberry paper and a 2" length of 3/8"-wide white paper for each one.

To make the five looped leaves, cut five 4-3/4" lengths of pale green paper, and mark sections on each one (as shown in the illustration at the bottom of the page) at 3/4", 1", 1-1/4", 1", and 3/4".

Shape each section into a loop, and glue the loops together.

Using the photo as a guide, cut a 3" length of pale green paper for the vine, and curl it slightly.

Glue the vine to the bag.

Arrange the leaves and flowers, and glue them to the bag.

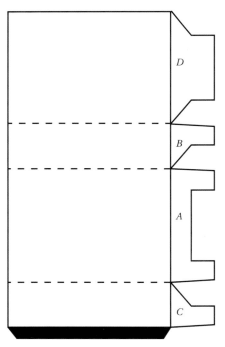

Enlarge by 206%

| 3/4" | 1" | 1-1/4" | 1" | 3/4" |

Fridge Magnets

The backs of these quilled miniatures have magnetic strips attached to them so that they'll hold messages and grocery lists to your refrigerator. Of course, the designs will add colorful accents to your kitchen, too.

Use narrow paper unless another width is specified. The instructions will yield one of each design.

Baskets

Weave a 4-1/2" x 1-1/4" rectangle, using narrow brown lengths for the horizontal strips and narrow tan lengths for the vertical strips. (For instructions on weaving paper, see page 29.)

Cut the three baskets from this woven rectangle, using the patterns as guides.

Fringed Flowers

Using 3" lengths of 1/4"-wide paper, make two cadet blue, three deep blue, and three brick fringed flowers.

Bunny Ear Flowers (make seven)

Glue together four pale peach 3" bunny ears.

Make a flower center by adding a brick 2" tight circle.

Leaves (make seventeen)

Cut a leaf shape from dark green paper, and curl it slightly.

Backgrounds

Using the photograph as a guide, cut a circle from brick sculpture paper, a square from fern green sculpture paper, and an oval from slate blue sculpture paper.

Cut these same three shapes from cardboard.

Glue a 1/2"-wide piece of gathered lace around the back of each piece of sculpture paper.

Glue a piece of cardboard to the sculpture paper so that the lace is sandwiched between.

Cut three 1" lengths from a magnetic strip, and glue one length to the back of each lace-edged shape.

• Assembly

First, curve the top center of each basket out slightly.

Then glue its sides and bottom to the background. (Glue Basket One to the brick background, Basket Two to the fern green background, and Basket Three to the slate blue background.)

Using the patterns as guides, arrange and glue two cadet blue fringed flowers and three bunny ear flowers in Basket One.

Glue three brick fringed flowers and two bunny ear flowers in Basket Two.

Glue three deep blue fringed flowers and two bunny ear flowers in Basket Three.

Add five or six leaves to each design.

Basket One

Basket Two

Basket Three

Quilling For Coasters

Coasters similar to the ones in which these charming designs are displayed can be purchased at many craft stores. These may be assembled in different ways, so be sure to read the instructions that come with them.

Coaster Number One

A double-rolling technique is used to make this design. Two strips are rolled simultaneously to make a loose circle. When the circle has expanded to the proper size, one of the strips will be a bit longer than the other. Trim the excess paper away before gluing the ends in place. (Use 1/8"-wide paper throughout.)

Large Flower

Place a length of antique red quilling paper on top of a length of pale dusty rose.

Double-roll and then shape two 3" curved petals.

Double-roll one 3" marquise with the same colors.

Glue the two petals to the marquise.

Add a 3" green crescent to the bottom of the flower.

Medium Flowers (make two)

Make this flower in the same way and with the same colors, but use 2" lengths to double-roll the two petals and one marquise, and add a 2" crescent at the bottom.

 Bud
Glue one sky blue 1" marquise to a 1" green crescent.

 Three-Flower Cluster (make two sky blue and one pale dusty rose)
Glue three 1" marquises to a 1" green crescent.

Stems and Scrolls

Using the pattern as a guide, cut various lengths of green paper, and curl the ends slightly, as required.

• Assembly

Glue the three flowers to the sides of the stems.

Add the scrolls, the bud, and the flower cluster.

Remove the adhesive cover from the coaster's insert, and press a piece of white paper over the base so that it sticks in place.

Trim off the excess paper.

Glue your quilled design to the white paper.

Place the insert into the coaster.

Remove the adhesive paper from the other side of the insert, and press the back onto it.

Coaster Number Two

Use narrow paper for all parts of this design.

Large Teardrop Flowers (make two)

To make each of the five petals, first glue a 2" length of soft ivory paper to a 1" length of coral, end to end.

Roll and shape a teardrop with each 3" length, starting with the soft ivory end.

Glue the five teardrops together.

 Small Teardrop Flowers (make two)

To make each of the five petals, glue a 1/2" length of soft ivory to a 1/2" length of pale peach, end to end.

With each 1" length, roll and shape a teardrop, beginning with the soft ivory end.

Glue the teardrops together.

 Small Rolled-Heart Flowers (make five)

Glue four coral 1" rolled hearts together.

Buds (make two)

Glue three coral 1" teardrops together.

Add a 1" soft ivory loose circle.

Stems and Scrolls

Using the pattern as a guide, cut various lengths of green paper, gently rolling the ends as required.

• Assembly

Glue a small pearl to the center of every flower.

Assemble the design components, using the pattern as a guide.

Then apply the design to the coaster's insert, following the instructions given with Coaster Number One.

Coaster Number Three

Use 1/8"-wide paper for all parts of this design.

Large Flower

Make two light blue 4" curved petals and one light blue 4" marquise.

Glue the three shapes together, using the pattern as a guide.

Add a green 3" crescent to the bottom of the assembled petals.

Medium Flower

Make two light blue 3" curved petals and one light blue 3" marquise.

Glue the petals together, and add a green 2" crescent.

 Small Rolled-Heart Flowers (make three)

Make three deep rose 1" rolled hearts, and glue them together.

 Marquise Flowers (make two)

Make five pink 1" marquises, and glue them together.

 Bunny Ear Flower

Make four white 1" bunny ear petals and one deep rose 3/4" loose circle to serve as the flower's center.

Glue the petals to the center.

Buds (make three)

Make one light blue 1" teardrop and one green 1" V scroll.

Glue the teardrop into the V scroll.

Leaves (make three)
Each leaf consists of a green
    1" teardrop.

Stems and Scrolls
Cut various lengths of green
    paper, using the pattern as
    a guide.

• Assembly
First assemble the complete
    design.
Then use the assembly instruc-
    tions given with Coaster
    Number One to insert the
    design into the coaster.

Quilling on Baskets

*Baskets make wonderful bases for quillwork; there
are literally hundreds of shapes and sizes from
which to choose. These were selected for the wide,
flat reeds running through their centers, reeds that
serve as perfect backgrounds.*

Pansy Design

Choose a basket with a wide, vertically placed reed for this design, unless you'd prefer to arrange the individual flowers horizontally. Feel free to make more flowers for a larger basket, but do use narrow paper for the entire design.

Large Pansy

To make the upper petal, fill in the outline with apricot 3" marquises.

For the two side petals, first place a bright yellow 1-1/2" crescent

over the crescent in the pattern. Then fill in the shaded areas of the patterns with rust 2" marquises and the unshaded areas with apricot 3" marquises.

To make the lower petal, first place a black 3" tight circle over the tight circle in the pattern.

Add a bright yellow 1-1/2" crescent, and then fill in the shaded area with rust 2" marquises and the unshaded area with apricot 3" marquises.

To assemble the pansy, gently curve and shape each petal first.

Then glue the side petals so that they overlap the upper petal; glue the lower petal so that it overlaps the side petals.

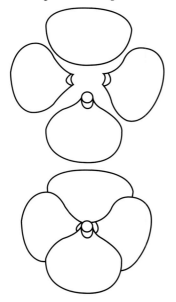

Small Pansies (make two)

Construct this flower as you did the large pansy, but use orange 3" marquises to fill in all four petals. Each side petal has a bright yellow 1-1/2" crescent, and the lower petal has a black 2" tight circle and a bright yellow 1-1/2" crescent.

Buds (make two)

Shape an apricot 5" irregular teardrop for the bud, using the pattern as a guide.

To make the calyx, cut points on one end of a few short strips of green paper, and curl each one. Glue several of these pointed strips to the bud.

Roll a green 5" grape roll, and glue it over the calyx.

Add a short green spiral as a stem.

Leaves (make a total of thirteen)

Make six leaves, each with three green 3" marquises. Make seven leaves, each with five green 3" marquises.

• Assembly

Using the photograph as a guide, position the three pansies on the basket, and glue them in place.

Add the leaves and buds.

Flowering Vine Design

This design is arranged horizontally, though there's no reason why you can't adapt it to run vertically instead. Use 1/8"-wide paper unless another width is specified.

Teardrop Flowers (make six)

Roll and glue together five brick 3" teardrops, and add a pale peach 2" loose circle to make the flower's center.

Fringed Flowers (make four)

Fringe a 4" length of cadet blue 3/8"-wide paper.

Leaves (make six sets)

Roll two dark green 2" teardrops. Cut a short length of dark green paper, and glue the two teardrops to it.

Bud Sprays (make six)

Using the pattern, cut a triangular shape from dark green 3/8"-wide (or wider) paper.

Roll this paper on the needle tool, beginning with the wide end of the triangle; glue the end down.

Cut four short lengths of dark green paper.

Glue two buds to each of two lengths and one bud to each of the other two lengths.

Bee

Roll a black 6" tight circle for the head and a black 4" teardrop for the body; glue these two shapes together.

Roll two gold 6" teardrops for the wings, and glue them to the bee at a slight angle so that their rounded ends are elevated.

Add a small black V for the antennae.

• Assembly

To make the vine, use the pattern as a guide to shape a length of dark green paper with a scroll on each end. You may adapt the length and shape of this strip to complement the size and shape of your basket, of course.

Glue the vine, on edge, to the basket's wide reed.

Position the flowers, and glue them to the basket.

Add the leaves and bud sprays.

Glue the bee above the flowers.

Woven Heart Border

A woven-paper heart (made with gold quill trim and adorned with half-pearls) lends a touch of timelessness to this sentimental border design.

Use 1/8"-wide paper unless another width is specified. The design will fit well on a 10" x 6-1/2" mat with a 5-1/2" x 3-1/2" rectangular opening. Place the mat in a 10" x 6-1/2" frame.

Woven Heart

Slip a sheet of graph paper under the wax paper on your quilling board.

Using the paper's lines as guides, weave a 2" x 2" square with gold quill trim. Space the gold lengths 1/8" apart. Each time a horizontal length crosses a vertical length, glue them together with a tiny drop of glue.

Glue the woven piece to a sheet of tan parchment paper.

Cut a heart shape from the glued sheets.

Create a border for the parchment-backed heart by gluing gold quill trim around it. Place the trim on edge, with its gold side facing in.

Glue another length of gold trim around the border, with its gold side facing out.

In each of the spaces between the woven gold lengths, glue a half-pearl.

Large Bunny Ear Flowers (make four)

Glue together four soft ivory 4" bunny ears.

To make the flower's center, add a soft green 4" tight circle.

Small Bunny Ear Flowers (make three)

Glue together four soft ivory 3" bunny ears.

Add a soft green 3" tight circle for the center.

Fringed Flowers (make eight)

Fringe a 3" length of 3/8"-wide teal paper, and roll it into a fringed flower.

Leaves

Cut four leaves from dark green 3/8"-wide paper, five leaves from celedon green 3/8"-wide paper, and four leaves from 3/8"-wide gold quill trim.

Fringe the leaves' edges, and curl each leaf slightly.

Double Scrolls (make five)

Tear a 3" length of dark green paper.

Fold it off-center, and roll a loose scroll on each end.

• Assembly

Arrange the group of shapes shown with the heart pattern (three bunny ear flowers, two fringed flowers, and five leaves) in the top left area of the mat, and glue them in place.

Add the other flowers, leaves, and scrolls, using the photograph as a guide.

Chess Board

Avid chess players and practiced quillers share at least two characteristics: patience and skill! This board took its designer seventeen hours to construct, but there's no doubt that it will provide its owner with a lifetime of pleasurable use. The intricate design is protected by a sheet of rigid plastic.

Board

If you don't have the tools to construct the mounting board itself, your local woodworking shop will do it for you. The inside dimensions are 15" x 15", and the top surface is surrounded by trim that creates a 1/4"-deep recess.

Use 1/8"-wide paper unless otherwise specified. Note that both the medallions can be quilled in any color combination. To copy this design exactly, use the photograph as a color guide; the colors used are ivory, tan, and brown.

Border Medallions (make thirty-six)

With a 12" length of paper, roll a 12" tight circle to make the medallion's center.

With 3" lengths in a contrasting color, roll eight tight circles and glue them around the center roll.

Roll eight marquises with 3" lengths of paper, and glue their points between the 3" tight circles.

Make eight 3" teardrops; arrange and glue them between the marquises, with their points facing out.

Playing Surface Medallions (make sixty-four)

As you make these medallions, note that the colors in thirty-two of them are the exact reverse of the colors in the other thirty-two.

To make the medallion's center, roll a 12" tight circle. (Remember to roll half of the required centers in one color and the other half in a contrasting color.)

Glue eight 3" tight circles around the center.

Roll four 6" marquises; position and glue them, using the pattern as a guide. Each one will reach into one corner of a square on the board.

Roll eight 6" teardrops to fill in the sides of each medallion, and glue them in place.

• Assembly

To guide you as you assemble the medallions on the board, measure and mark 1-1/2"-square sections on the board's top surface. Then arrange the assembled medallions, alternating their color placement as illustrated in the photograph.

Have a 1/8"-thick piece of plexiglass cut to fit the board's recess, and drop it gently in place.

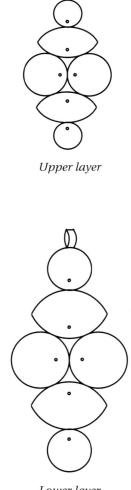

Upper layer

Lower layer

Use 1/8"-wide paper for both designs.

Deep Rose Earrings
(make two, using upper layer pattern only)

Using deep rose paper, roll the following shapes:
two 6" eccentric loose circles,
two 3" eccentric loose circles,
two 6" eccentric fans,
one 1" teardrop, and
two 2" tight circles.

Glue the eccentric shapes together, using the pattern as a guide.

Slip a jump ring through the teardrop.

Glue the teardrop to the top loose circle, taking care to place it on its side.

Add the two tight circles on either side of the teardrop.

Teal and Turquoise Earrings (make two)

Lower Layer

Using teal paper, roll the following shapes: two 9" eccentric circles, two 9" eccentric fans, two 6" eccentric circles, and one 1" teardrop.

Using the pattern, glue the eccentric shapes together.

Slip a jump ring through the teardrop.

Glue the teardrop to the top loose circle, positioning the teardrop on its side.

Upper Layer

Using turquoise paper, roll the following eccentric shapes: two 6" circles, two 6" fans, and two 3" circles.

Glue these shapes together.

• Assembly

Center the upper layer over the lower layer, and glue it in place.

Earrings

Quilled earrings are everything but waterproof: they look great, feel light and breezy as they dangle from your ears, and can be made in any number of styles. These examples feature eccentric shapes.

A smile
can never be kept:
It can only be
given away

Oval Border

Select a favorite poem or a treasured photograph, and set it off with this lovely border. A double mat will complement the flowers' colors and allow light and shade to accent the layered shapes.

Use 1/8"-wide paper unless another width is specified.

Double Marquise Flower

Glue together seven white 7" marquises for the bottom layer.

For the top layer, glue together seven white 6" marquises.

Then glue the two layers together, staggering them so that the petals in the bottom layer are visible between those in the top layer.

Make the flower's center by adding a pale green 5" tight circle.

Large Single Marquise Flowers (make five)

Glue together five raspberry 6" marquises.

To create the flower's center, roll a 5" length of silver quill trim into a tight circle, and then glue the circle (on its side) to the flower.

Small Single Marquise Flowers (make four)

Glue together five white 4" marquises.

Add a 3" pale green tight circle for the flower's center.

Bunny Ear Flowers (make six)

Glue together four white 4" bunny ears.

Add a white 3" tight circle for the flower's center.

Fringed Flowers (make six)

Glue a 3" length of 1/8"-wide raspberry paper to a 3" length of 3/8"-wide silver quill trim, end to end.

Beginning with the raspberry end, roll this 6" length into a fringed flower.

Bud Sprays (make four)

Roll three raspberry tight circles, using 1", 2", and 3" lengths.

Position the tight circles on a short, curved length of green paper, with the smallest one at the tip, and glue them in place.

Scrolls (make six)

Roll a celedon green 3" loose scroll.

Spirals (make three)

Roll a spiral with a short length of celedon green paper.

Leaves (make nine)

Cut a leaf from 3/8"-wide, dark green paper.

Fringe the edges and curl the leaf slightly.

• Assembly

Select an 8" x 10" double oval mat with a 6" x 4-3/4" opening. (If you've selected a verse for the interior, one to which you can glue the overlapping quilled shapes, glue it behind the mat at this point. If you plan to use a photo, however, first assemble the quilled border on the mat, gluing the overlapping sections to the shapes nearest to them, and then fit the photo behind the mat.)

Glue three leaves to the back of the double marquise flower.

Glue one or two leaves behind each of the small single marquise flowers.

Glue a bud spray to four of the large single marquise flowers.

Glue a scroll to each of the bunny ear flowers.

Glue a spiral to three of the fringed flowers.

Position the double marquise flower first, and glue it to the mat.

Arrange the other flowers, and glue them in place.

Quilled Flower Hat

All the warmth and pleasure of spring are reflected in the delicate, airy quillwork and dainty ribbon on this miniature hat. Pastel colors and loosely rolled shapes complement the open weave of the hat itself.

Use 1/8"-wide paper unless another width is specified.

Large Center Flower

To make the lower layer, glue together five soft ivory 6" teardrops.

Glue five soft ivory 4" teardrops together to make the upper layer.

Position the upper layer on the lower layer so that each petal in the upper layer rests between two petals in the lower layer, and glue the layers together.

Add a pearl to make the flower's center.

Marquise Flowers (make two)

Glue six soft ivory 4" marquises together.

Add a 1" coral loose circle for the flower's center.

Large Teardrop Flowers (make two)

Glue five pale peach 4" teardrops together.

Add a pearl for the flower's center.

Medium Teardrop Flowers (make two)

To make each of the five petals, first glue a 2" length of soft ivory to a 1" length of coral, end to end.

Beginning with the pale ivory end, roll a teardrop.

Glue five teardrops together to make one flower.

Add a pearl to make the flower's center.

 Large Fringed Flowers (make two pale peach and two sky blue)

Make a fringed flower from a 4" piece of 5/8"-wide paper.

 Medium Fringed Flowers (make two pale peach and three coral)

Make a fringed flower from a 4" length of 3/8"-wide paper.

 **Lily of the Valley Sprays (make two sky blue and two pale peach)**

Using 1" lengths of paper, make three bunny ears, and glue them to a curved green 2" length.

Fern Leaves (make eleven)

Cut a leaf shape from 3/8"-wide green paper.

Fringe the leaf's edges, and then curl it slightly.

Scrolls

Roll six green 2" loose scrolls, using narrow paper.

• Assembly

Glue a piece of 3/8"-wide ribbon around the bottom of the hat's crown.

Make a bow, and wire it to the hat's brim, near the ribbon.

Glue the center flower to the top of the bow.

Arrange the flowers, leaves, and scrolls, using the photograph as a guide, and glue them in place.

Quilled Nosegay
for a Bentwood Box

Distinctly Victorian in flavor, this delicate, lace-framed nosegay transforms a simple container into an heirloom gift box. Two design elements accentuate the three-dimensional appearance: the use of very wide paper for the fringed flowers and the elevation of some shapes on hidden pegs. You can also place this nosegay design in a 6" round frame.

Use 1/8"-wide paper unless another width is specified.

Large Flowers (make three)

To make the flower's center, first glue together a soft ivory 6" length and a pale green 2" length, end to end.

Then, beginning with the soft ivory end, roll an inverted grape roll.

To make petals, roll eleven soft ivory 6" narrow ovals. Shape these as you would marquises, but round the ends rather than pinching them into sharp points.

Glue the petals to the flower's center to form the lower layer.

Roll eleven soft ivory 5-1/2" narrow ovals, and glue these to the center to form the upper layer. (To give the flower its saucer-like shape, be sure to position several of these petals at angles and to glue most with their outer ends raised.)

Fringed Flowers (make six)

Using a 4" length of 5/8"-wide soft ivory paper, roll a fringed flower.

The three, angled, fringed flowers that are positioned on the arrangement's outer edges need calyxes. (Omit calyxes on the other three fringed flowers; their upright positions hide what lies beneath them.) For each calyx, cut five or six short pointed lengths from pale green paper, and curve the pointed ends.

Glue the calyxes to the three fringed flowers' bases.

Roll a pale green 6" grape roll, and glue it just below the calyx.

Fringed Buds (make three)

Cut a 3" length of 5/8"-wide soft ivory paper.

Mark 1" sections along its length, as shown in the pattern on the next page.

Trim the first section to a 1/8" width and the center section to a 3/8" width.

Fringe the 3/8" and 5/8" sections.

To curve the fringed 5/8"-wide section inward, hold the fringed paper horizontally along your thumb, and curl it by pressing its length with a needle tool.

Beginning with the 1/8" section, roll this 3" length as though you were rolling a tight circle. (Roll toward the inside of the curved section. This will create a fringed flower with fringed ends that curve toward the center.)

Add a calyx and grape roll, just as you did for the three, angled, fringed flowers.

Teardrop Flowers (make three)

Glue five soft ivory 4" teardrops together, with their points facing out and angled upward.

Using narrow pale green paper, roll five or six 1/2" loose scrolls.

Glue these into a cluster in the flower's center.

Buds on Stems

Make three sets of five bunny ears; each set should include two soft ivory 2"; two soft ivory 2-1/2"; and one soft ivory 3".

Glue each set of five bunny ears to a curved length of pale green paper, arranging them with the smallest bunny ears at the ends.

Make one set of nine bunny ears: three soft ivory 2"; three soft ivory 2-1/2"; and three soft ivory 3".

Glue this set to a curved length of pale green paper, once again arranging the buds by size.

Greenery (make six)

Roll six pale green tight circles: one 1", two 1-1/2", two 2", and one 2-1/2".

Along a short curved length of pale green paper, arrange and glue these circles by size, with the smallest tight circle at one end.

Leaves (make approximately seventeen)

Cut a leaf from 3/8"-wide pale green paper.

Fringe its edges, and then curve the leaf slightly.

Lace-Trimmed Background

Cut a 2-1/2"-diameter circle from poster board to serve as the nosegay's base.

Pleat a 1-1/4"-wide, 16"-long piece of lace into a circle.

Glue the strip to the base, overlapping the base's edge by 1/4".

• Assembly

Using the assembly guide and photograph, position the three large flowers. In order to raise them, add single or double pegs to each one before gluing it to the base.

Position and glue the other flowers in the same way.

Attach some of the leaves below the large and fringed flowers to give depth to the arrangement and to conceal the cardboard circle.

Add the bunny ear buds, greenery, and the rest of the leaves as filler. Position most of these shapes around the edge; place a few between and overlapping the center flowers.

Glue the nosegay and base to the top of a painted 5" bentwood box.

Arrangement of large flowers

Fringed bud pattern

Border for a Quilling Verse

This verse expresses the sentiments of every avid quiller. The teal and orchid floral border that frames it is one of many border styles that can be adapted to suit this poem or others.

Use 1/8"-wide paper unless another width is specified.

Double Teardrop Flowers (make two)
Glue together five teal 6" teardrops for the lower layer and five teal 5" teardrops for the upper layer.
Glue the upper layer to the lower layer.
Add a white 3" tight circle for the flower's center.

Large Teardrop Flowers (make four)
Glue together five teal 4" teardrops.
Add a white 3" tight circle for the flower's center.

Small Teardrop Flowers (make three)
Glue together five teal 3" teardrops.
Add a white 2" tight circle for the flower's center.

Large Marquise Flowers (make two)
Glue together six orchid 5" marquises.
Add a raspberry 3" loose circle for the flower's center.

Small Marquise Flowers (make five)
Glue together five orchid 3" marquises.
Add a raspberry 2" loose circle for the flower's center.

Buds (make three)
Glue an orchid 2" marquise into a green 3" V scroll.
Add a short length of green for a stem.

Bud Sprays (make seven)
Roll three green tight circles, using 1", 2", and 3" lengths.
Glue the tight circles (arranged by size) on a short curved length of green paper, with the smallest tight circle at the tip.

Leaves (make seventeen)
Cut these from 3/8"-wide green paper and fringe them.

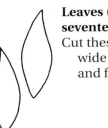

Scrolls
Cut four green strips to the following lengths: 12", 10", 7", and 5".
Roll a very loose scroll on each end of each strip.
Curve the strips to resemble those shown in the photo.

• Assembly
First, using the photo as a guide, position and glue the four scrolls along the sides, top, and bottom of the verse.
Then arrange the quilled flowers and greenery, and glue them in place.

Assembly guide for project on page 116.
Enlarge by 231%.

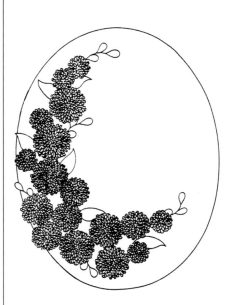

I've tried most all the handcrafts
That require coordination ᗭ;
I've stitched and sketched and decoupaged
And made my own creation ᗭ.

But never had I found a craft
That made each moment thrilling
Until I found these paper strips
And Started doing Quilling. ✝

—Ken Brown
©1975

Floral Border for an Oval Frame

This charming border pattern features fringed flowers, some made with 5/8"-wide paper and others with 3/8"-wide paper. Select any colors you like. The design in the photograph includes lilac, turquoise, pale pink, ivory, cadet blue, and deep blue.

Small Fringed Flowers (make six)
Use 3" lengths of 3/8"-wide paper.

Medium Fringed Flowers (make five)
Use 4" lengths of 5/8"-wide paper.

Large Fringed Flowers (make four)
Use 6" lengths of 5/8"-wide paper.

Duo-Tone Fringed Flowers (make two)
Place two 3" lengths of fringed 5/8"-wide paper (in contrasting colors) flat against each other, and roll them into a tight circle.
Shape the tight circle into a fringed flower.

Stems and Quilled Leaves
Roll thirteen green 3" teardrops.
Cut five short lengths of green paper to serve as stems, and glue two or three leaves to each one.

Cut-Out Leaves
Cut five or six leaves from green 3/8"-wide paper.
Fringe the edges of each leaf, and then curl the ends slightly.

• Assembly
Position the flowers and glue them in place, letting some overlap the oval frame.
Add the leaves.

See assembly guide on page 114.

Free-Standing
Quilled Clown

Jinisans, *named for their creator, Virginia Alexander,
are three-dimensional paper representations of
people. They range from 2" to 4" in height and
can be as simple, ornate, or unusual as you like.*

Use 1/4"-wide paper unless
another width is specified.
Fill all open cavities with rolled
paper, dried glue, or a similar
material to prevent hollow
pieces from collapsing and
to afford a base on which to
glue other parts.

Head

To make the clown's face, first
glue two 24" lengths of white
paper together, end to end.

Roll a tight circle with this 48"
length.

Shape the circle to make one
surface convex by easing it
over a rounded object; keep
the convex surface as smooth
as possible.

Repeat with a 48" length of 1/8"-
wide paper to make the back
of the head.

To stabilize the shapes, coat their
inside surfaces with glue.

Glue the front and back of the
head together, placing a rolled
piece of paper between the two
pieces before doing so.

Body

Glue two 24" lengths and one
12" length of light blue paper
together, end to end.

With this 60" length, roll a tight
circle.

Using the point of a pencil, carefully push the circle's center
upward to form a 1-1/2"-high
cone shape. Flatten the cone's
point slightly.

Coat the cone's inside surface
with glue.

Arms (make two)

Roll a light blue 18" length of
paper into a tight circle.

Shape the circle into a 1-1/4"-
long cone shape, using the
same technique that you
used to make the body.

Coat the inside of the shape
with glue.

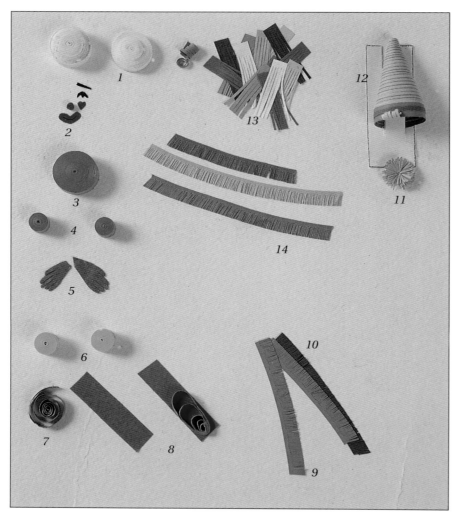

1. head (front and back); 2. facial features; 3. coil for body; 4. coils for arms;
5. hands; 6. coils for legs; 7. coil for shoe; 8. top and bottom of shoe;
9. fringe to trim shoes; 10. fringe to trim neckline; 11. pompom for back of hat;
12. double coil pushed out to form hat; 13. fringe for hair;
14. fringe for pompom buttons

leaving enough paper at the wrist ends to insert these shapes into the sleeves.

Cut fingers in each mitten shape.

Hat

Place one 24" length of yellow paper on top of one 24" length of light blue paper.

Pull the yellow length back so that about 1/4" of the blue shows at the end of the layered lengths.

Glue the overlapped ends to each other.

Roll the two lengths into a tight circle, starting with the blue end and holding the blue length a little above the yellow so that a thin border shows.

From the yellow side of the tight circle, using the same technique as for the body, shape the circle into a 1-1/4"-high cone.

Coat the inside surface with glue.

Trim the bottom border with a narrow length of orange paper.

Assembly of Main Parts

Glue the head to the top of the body, the legs to the shoes, and the hands into the arms.

Bend the right arm, taking care not to let it uncoil.

Glue the legs into the body cavity.

Glue the arms to the body's sides and to the point where the head and body meet.

Facial Features, Collar, and Hair

Roll a 1/2" length of 1/16"-wide red paper into a tight circle for the nose.

To cover the end of the nose, glue red paper to one end of the tight circle.

When the glue has dried, carefully cut the excess paper away.

Position the nose so that it covers the hole in the face's center, and glue it in place.

Cut a red paper mouth, about 3/8" long, and glue it in place.

Use a thin-nibbed pen to mark the mouth opening. (Check to

Legs (make two)

Roll an 18" length of yellow paper into a tight circle.

Shape this circle just as you shaped the body.

Coat the inside surface with glue.

Shoes (make two)

Roll a dark green 8" loose circle, about 1/2" in diameter, and form a shoe shape with it.

Glue the shape onto a piece of 3/8"-wide orange paper.

Put glue on the shoe's top surface, and place another piece of 3/8"-wide orange paper on top.

When the glue has dried, very carefully trim the excess orange paper from around the shoe's edges.

Hands (make two)

Glue the flat surfaces of two pieces of 3/8"-wide orange paper together.

Cut mitten shapes for the hands,

make sure that the ink won't bleed.)

Cut two red hearts, each about 1/8"-wide, and glue them onto the cheeks.

Cut two black eyes, each 3/16" across, and glue them in place.

Cut two black eyebrows, each about 1/2" long, and glue them in position.

Fringe a 3-1/2" length of dark blue paper.

Wrap the solid edge of the fringed piece around the neck, overlapping its ends; glue it in place. Spread the fringes out toward the body.

To make the hair, first cut about twenty-five to thirty 1" lengths of 1/4"-wide yellow, dark and light green, dark and light blue, and orange paper.

Fringe the 1/4" ends of all these pieces, and then set aside seven or eight of them.

Roll the other fringed pieces from their fringed ends toward their solid ends, and glue them closed.

In the same fashion, fringe and roll the pieces that you set aside, but don't glue them closed. Instead, glue these to the hat's inside front edge, with their curled sections outside the hat's edge.

Place the hat on the head, use a pencil to lightly mark its position, and then remove the hat.

Glue the other hair pieces to the head, below the marked line and in random order so that they frame the face and extend down to the collar in back. (Try to cover all white spots on the head's back.)

Place the hat on the head, adjust the hair, and glue the hat in place.

Pompoms

Roll six 3" lengths of fringed paper (one orange, two dark blue, two dark green, and one light green) into fringed flower shapes.

Glue each pompom in place as shown in the photograph.

Balloon

Glue two 24" lengths of 1/8"-wide light blue paper together, end to end.

Roll the 48" length into a tight circle. Gently push on its center to form half the balloon.

Repeat with two 1/8"-wide lengths of orange paper.

Cut a 5" length of floral wire.

Bend one end into a small loop.

Insert the wire's straight end through the inside center of the balloon bottom, and draw the wire through so that the loop rests in the concave shape.

Glue some stuffing into the balloon halves, and then glue the top half to the bottom half.

Cut a length of purple paper, and glue it around the balloon's center.

Cut a length of 1/8"-wide green paper; center and glue it on top of the purple length.

Hold the balloon next to the clown's head.

Fit the wire into the clown's hand, and draw it down to rest on the "floor."

Glue the balloon to the side of the clown's head.

Bend the hand around the wire, and glue it in place.

Cut the end of the wire, leaving about 1/3" to help balance the clown. If your clown won't stand on his own, make a standard by rolling a large tight circle, and glue the clown's shoes to it.

Spray the entire figure with a non-yellowing waterproofing or fixing spray.

To dust the figure, use a soft paint brush.

You may not want to let youngsters play with Jinisans; the figures are surprisingly hardy, but their parts can be harmful if swallowed!

Quilled Miniatures

Quilled miniatures take a bit of care, but don't let that stop you from trying your hand at these astonishing projects. Be patient and think tiny! (These projects are scaled 1" to one foot.) You'll love the results.

To secure flower stems into containers, you may use one of two methods. Either place filler in the container (a mixture of sand and craft glue), and insert the greenery before the filler dries, or roll a loose circle, glue it into the bottom of the container, and glue the stems between the circle's loops.

Miniature Plants on Shelves

The instructions that follow are given to match the plants on the shelves, clockwise from top left. Use 1/8"-wide paper unless another width is specified.

Airplane Plant

Container
This is a 1/2"-tall miniature basket with a 3/4" opening.

Leaves
Cut twenty-two strips of narrow green paper, ranging from 5/8" to 1-5/8" in length.
Trim one end of each leaf into a

long point, and curve each leaf slightly.

Cut eleven pieces of narrow soft ivory paper in various lengths.

Cut each of these in half lengthwise, trim one end to a long point, and glue one down the center of each leaf.

Runners

Begin with two lengths of soft ivory narrow paper.

Cut each of these in half lengthwise.

Trim the four pieces to lengths ranging from 1-1/4" to 1-3/4", and curve one end of each into a U-shape so that it will drape over the edge of the basket.

Make twelve small leaves (following the preceding leaf-making instructions), but make these in lengths ranging from 5/16" to 3/8".

Glue two or three of these short leaves to the ends of the runners.

• Assembly

Glue the leaves into the basket, curving the ends of some so that they'll hang over the basket's edge. Be sure to position each leaf so that the soft ivory strip is visible from the front of the basket.

Glue the runners into the basket, adjusting their curves so that each runner can be seen clearly.

Blooming Bells (make two)

Container

Shape an orange 24" grape roll into a flower pot.

Greenery

Roll thirty to forty loose scrolls, using 1/2" lengths of narrow green paper.

Flowers (make six)

Glue a 1" length of bright white narrow paper to a 2" length of crimson narrow paper.

Roll this 3" length into a grape roll, beginning with the white end.

• Assembly

Fill each pot with filler to just below its lip.

Add the loose scrolls in a mound on the filler, placing a few so that they hang down over the edge of the pot.

Glue the flowers to the greenery.

Hyacinths (pot of three)

Container

Shape a 48" orange grape roll into a flower pot.

Flowers (make one each of cadet blue, lilac, and white)

Roll approximately eighteen loose scrolls, using 1/2" lengths of narrow paper.

Make a flower stem by cutting a 1" length of floral wire and spreading glue on 5/8" of it.

Roll the wire's glued end in the loose scrolls so that the scrolls cluster on the wire.

Leaves

Cut eighteen pieces of narrow green paper in lengths ranging from 3/8" to 1".

Trim one end of each leaf to a point, and curl that end slightly.

• Assembly

Glue the flower stems into the pot.

Add the leaves so that they curve in different directions, placing the longer pieces toward the back.

Single Hyacinth

Follow the preceding directions, but make the pot with a 24"

length, use only lilac paper, cut the floral wire stem to 7/8", and make only thirteen leaves.

Trailing Sedum

Container

Shape a rust 24" grape roll into a flower pot.

Leaves

Cut five pieces of wire: three 1/4"-long, one 1"-long, and one 1/2"-long.

Make twenty small fringed leaves, using 3/8"-wide paper.

Fold each leaf in half lengthwise.

Bend the 1/2" and 1" wires over so that they'll hang over the pot's edge.

Glue seven leaves to the 1" wire and three leaves to the 1/2" wire; be sure that they cover the wires.

Glue two leaves to each of the 1/4" wires.

Glue the remaining leaves into the pot.

• Assembly

Glue the leaf-covered wires into the pot.

Use the remaining leaves to fill the pot.

Long-Stemmed Lilies

Container

To make the bottom half, glue two brown 24" lengths together, end to end, and roll a 48" grape roll.

To make the top half, first glue a brown 24" length to a brown 21" length.

Then roll this 45" length on a round, 1-8"-thick dowel, gluing the paper after the first wrap.

Remove the tight circle from the dowel, and shape it into a grape roll.

Glue the two halves together.

Flowers (make three)

Cut out (or punch out, with a star-shaped punch) three stars from 5/8"-wide brick paper.

Clip one point from each star.

Make a three-pointed cone shape by overlapping the two points on either side of the missing point. Glue one point (the shaded point shown in the illustration) behind the one that overlaps it.

Use a needle tool to curl back the three petals.

Make a fringed flower, using a 1" length of 1/4"-wide soft ivory paper.

Glue this flower inside the three-pointed cone.

To make a stem, glue a 2" length of floral wire to the flower.

Leaves

Cut five pieces of green narrow paper, ranging from 1-1/8" to 2" in length.

Trim the end of each piece to a long point.

• Assembly

Trim the flower stems to 1-1/4", 1-1/2", and 2".

Arrange the flowers in the container, with the shortest flower bent forward slightly.

Arrange the leaves around the flowers.

Quilled Dinnerware

Use narrow paper unless another width is specified.

All of these pieces are made in a similar fashion. The plate and saucer are shaped by curving the edges of tight circles just slightly upward. The other pieces are made with grape

rolls. To keep the shapes from collapsing, coat their least visible surfaces—the entire bottom of the plate and saucer, and the inner surfaces of all other shapes—with glue.

The following instructions include the lengths for each grape roll. Use narrow paper unless another width is specified, and always begin rolling with the first color listed. Handles are made by curving short lengths of red paper. Glue component shapes together when appropriate.

Plate (tight circle): 12" red, 24" white, 24" white, and 12" red

Saucer (tight circle): 24" white and 3" red

Cup (grape roll): 20" white and 3" red

Teapot

Base (grape roll): 18" red

Bottom Half (grape roll): 24" white and 18" white

Top Half (grape roll): 5" white, 1" red, 24" white, and 12" white

Spout: Roll a 1" length of 1/8"-wide paper into a tight spiral, the edges of which overlap. Remove the spiral from the tool, hold it securely, and spread glue on its inner surface. Curve the spiral slightly, and flatten the end that attaches to the teapot.

Knob: add a red 1" tight circle.

Creamer

Base (grape roll): 12" red

Bowl (grape roll): 24" white and 3" red. Pinch a spout on one edge with a pair of tweezers.

Sugar Bowl

Base (grape roll): 12" red

Bottom (grape roll): 24" white and 3" red

Lid (shallow grape roll): 24" white and 3" red

Knob: Add a 2" red tight circle.

Covered Pedestal Bowl

Base (grape roll): 16" white and 4" red

Bowl (grape roll): 12" red, 24" white, and 6" red

Lid (grape roll): 12" red, 24" white, and 6" red

Knob: Add a red 2" tight circle.

Vase

Base (grape roll): 16" white, using 1/8"-wide paper

Top (tall, conical grape roll): 24" white, using 1/8"-wide paper

Flowers and Leaves: Roll three fringed flowers, using 3" lengths of pink 1/8"-wide paper. To make stems, glue a short length of floral wire to each flower. Cut narrow, pointed lengths from green 1/8"-wide paper, and curve each one slightly.

Rose Bouquet

Container
This container is a white, 3/8"-high bowl with a 1/2" opening.

Roses
Make seven red and five white folded roses, using 1/8"-wide paper.
(See pages 30 and 31 for further instructions.)
Cut twelve wires, ranging in length from 3/4" to 1-3/8".
Glue a wire to each completed rose.

Leaves
From green 3/8"-wide paper, cut out seven leaves with stems and twenty-three leaves without stems.
Glue two stemless leaves to each stemmed leaf (one on each side of the stem) to make leaf clusters.
Glue a leaf cluster to each of three rose stems; glue the single leaves to the remaining rose stems.
Glue four leaf clusters to short lengths of wire.

• Assembly
Arrange the roses in the pot.
Fill in the bare spots with the leaf clusters on wires.

Carousel Horses

*Youngsters will love these exciting quilled horses.
While one prances in what must be perfect time
to the music, the other, with its flying mane, looks
as if it's ready to gallop right off the carousel.*

Use 1/8"-wide paper unless
 another width is specified.

Carousel Horse Number One

Body and Body Details
Fill in the body pattern on page 126
 with white 2-1/2" marquises.
Add a black 4" irregularly shaped
 square for the hoof.
Roll an 8" tight circle for the eye,
 letting it expand just enough to
 be shaped into a tight oval.
Roll a white 8" teardrop for the
 front ear and a white 4"
 teardrop for the back ear.
Cut approximately fifteen
 irregular shapes from 3/8"-
 wide white paper to make up
 the mane.
Make one or two curved cuts
 in each shape, and then curve
 the shapes slightly.

Saddle, Breast Collar, and Bridle

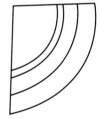

The four saddle shapes are cut
 to overlap one another; the
 largest shape, in other words,
 is as large as the entire pattern.
 Using the photo as a color
 guide, cut the four shapes from
 pink, rose, light blue, and slate
 blue sculpture paper.
Glue the four pieces together,
 layering them as you do.

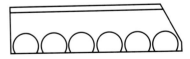

The two breast collar strips are
 also cut to overlap each other.
 Cut the wide strip from rose
 sculpture paper and the

narrow strip from light blue sculpture paper.

Glue the narrow shape on top of the wide shape.

With a 1/4" hole punch, punch six circles from pink paper.

Cut a flat section on each circle, and using the pattern as a guide, glue them to the breast collar.

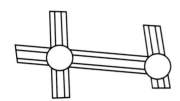

To make the bridle, first cut three narrow lengths of light blue sculpture paper and three wider lengths from slate blue paper.

Then glue the light blue strips to the slate blue strips.

Punch two circles from slate blue paper, using a 1/4" hole punch, and set them aside, along with the bridle strips.

Make each of the four tassels by cutting a 6" strip of narrow cadet blue and marking it at every 1/2" point along its length.

Then fold it, accordion-style, at each mark.

Wrap the top of the accordion shape with a length of sky blue paper, and glue the wrapper down securely.

• **Assembly**

Using the pattern on page 127 as a guide, glue the breast collar and saddle to the horse.

Position and glue the three bridle strips, and then add the two circles over the points where the strips intersect.

Add the tassels.

Position the eye and ears, and glue them in place.

Add a tiny dot of white paint to the center of the eye.

Glue two of the mane shapes in front of the near ear.

Beginning near the saddle, glue the rest of the mane pieces to the horse, overlapping them as shown in the pattern.

Carousel Horse Number Two

Body and Body Details

Fill in the body pattern with white 2-1/2" marquises.

To make the hoof, add two grey 3-1/2" irregularly shaped

Horse Number One

Horse Number Two

triangles and one grey 3"
irregularly shaped marquise.
Roll a white 6" teardrop for the
ear.
From 3/8"-wide paper, cut
approximately seventeen of the
irregular shapes that make up
the mane. Use the pattern on
page 127 as a guide when cutting these shapes.
Make one or two curved cuts
in each shape, and then
curve the shapes slightly.

**Saddle, Collar, Breast Collar,
Bridle, and Reins**

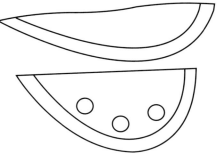

Cut the four shapes for the
saddle, two for the top section
and two for the bottom
section, from pink and rose
sculpture paper. (Note that
one shape in each set is as
large as the entire pattern;
the other shape in each set
overlaps the larger shape.)
Glue two pieces together to form
each of the two saddle sections.

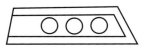

Cut the two collar shapes from
light blue and slate blue
sculpture paper.

Cut the breast collar from rose
sculpture paper.

the collar, four to the breast collar, and one to the bridle.
Glue a jewel in place for the eye.
Position the ear; then glue it in place.
Glue two of the mane shapes in front of the ear.
Beginning near the saddle, glue the rest of the mane to the horse, overlapping the shapes as shown in the pattern.
Cut a 1/4" dowel to a length that's appropriate for the size of mat you intend to use.
Paint the dowel with gold paint. When the paint has dried, glue the dowel to the background, as shown in the photo.
Elevate the horse by gluing two pegs to its back; make these with 1/4"-wide white paper.
Position the horse, and glue the pegs to the background.
Cut 1/8"-wide lengths of satin ribbons, one rose and one slate blue, for trim.
Using the photo as a guide, glue one end of each ribbon behind the horse and the other end onto the dowel.

To make the bridle, cut two narrow lengths of light blue sculpture paper and two wider lengths from slate blue paper.
Glue the light blue strip to the slate blue strip, and set the pieces aside.
With a 1/4" hole punch, punch a circle from slate blue paper, and set it aside.

• Assembly
Using the pattern as a guide, glue the saddle, breast collar, collar, and bridle strips to the horse.
Glue the slate blue circle to the point where the bridle strips intersect.
Glue three jewels to the lower section of the saddle, three to

For Kids to Quill!

With just a little help from an adult quiller, any child can make these projects. Teach your youngster how to roll the basic shapes (on a toothpick, not on a needle quilling tool), point out the photos, and then let go! Patterns may not be necessary; some children will use familiar shapes to create designs of their own.

Bubbles: black 1-1/2", 1", and 1/2" tight circles
Glue the body, tail, and fins together.
Add the eye.
Glue the fish to the bookmark, and then add the air bubbles.

Use 1/8"-wide paper for every design. When you come to a list of shapes in the instructions, go ahead and make them; the instructions will tell you when to glue them together.

Bookmarks

Fish
Body: orange 12" marquise
Tail: orange 4" crescent
Fins: two orange 2" marquises
Eye: black 1" tight circle

Lilac Flower
Flower petals: five lilac 3" teardrops
Flower center: white 3" tight circle
Leaf: green 2" marquise
Stem: green 2" loose scroll
Glue the petals together and add the tight circle for the center.

Glue the leaf to the stem, and then glue the stem between two of the petals.

Position and glue the assembly on the bookmark.

Blue Flower

Petals: five cadet blue 3" teardrops

Flower center: deep blue 3" tight circle

Scrolls: two deep blue (1" and 2") loose scrolls

Glue the petals to the flower center.

Glue the flower in place on the bookmark, and then add the scrolls.

Picture

First make the shapes for the caterpillar, mouse, butterfly, and bee. Keep the shapes in separate piles so that you don't mix them up! Then, using the photograph as a guide, glue each pile of shapes together.

Caterpillar

Body: six soft green 3" tight circles

Head: soft green 5" tight circle

Antennae: tiny soft green V

Mouse

Body: grey 9" teardrop

Head: grey 3" teardrop

Ear: grey 2" teardrop

Foot: grey 1-1/2" teardrop

Nose: black 1" tight circle

Tail: grey 1-1/2" loose scroll

Butterfly

Body: gold 3" marquise

Antennae: gold 1" V scroll

Wing parts (large): two yellow 3" teardrops

Wing parts (small): two yellow 1-1/2" teardrops

Bee

Body: black 3" teardrop
Head: black 3" tight circle
Antennae: tiny black V
Wings: two gold 3" teardrops

The flowers are described from left to right, just as they appear in the photo. Make the shapes for each flower, and then assemble it.

Flower One

Buds: two orchid 1-1/2" teardrops
Scrolls: two green 1-1/2" V scrolls
Long stem: green 1-1/4" length
Short stem: green 3/4" length
Looped leaves: green 2-1/2" length, looped twice

Glue one bud into each scroll; then glue the scrolls to the stems.
Glue the stems together, and then add the looped leaves.

Flower Two

Petals: five blue 2-1/2" teardrops
Flower center: bright white 2-1/2" tight circle
Stem: green 1" length
Leaf: green 2" marquise

Glue the petals together, and then add the flower center on top.
Glue the leaf to the stem and the stem to the flower.

Flower Three

Flowers: three yellow 2" open hearts
Stem: green 2" length, slightly curved
Long leaf: green 1-1/2" length, with one pointed end
Short leaf: green 1" length, with one pointed end

Glue the flowers and leaves to the stem.

Flower Four

Flower petals: three orchid 2" teardrops
Bud: one orchid 2" teardrop
Scrolls: two green 1-1/2" V scrolls
Looped leaves: one green 1-1/2" length, looped once; one green 2-1/2" length, looped twice
Long stem: green 2" length
Short stem: green 1/2" length

Glue the petals into one of the scrolls, and glue the bud into the other scroll.
Glue the scrolls and looped leaves to the stems.

Flower Five

Petals: five cadet blue 2" teardrops
Flower center: bright white 2" tight circle
Stem: green 3/4" length, slightly curved
Leaf: green 2" marquise

Glue the petals together first, and then add the flower center.
Glue the leaf to the stem and the stem to the flower.

• Assembly

Glue all the shapes to the background, using the photograph as a guide.

Border for a School Picture

Butterfly Body
Body: black 3" marquise
Head: black 2" marquise
Antennae: black 1" V scroll

Butterfly Wings (make two)
First, glue together a 2" length of cadet blue, a 3" length of bright yellow, and a 3" length of gold, end to end.

Then roll a loose circle with this 8"-long strip, beginning with the cadet blue end. Shape a teardrop from it.

Glue together a 2" length of bright yellow and a 3" length of gold.

Roll a loose circle with the 5" length, beginning with the bright yellow end, and then shape a teardrop from it.

• Butterfly Assembly
Glue the head to the body first, and then add the wings.

Glue the antennae on last.

Large Flower
Petals: six turquoise 4" marquises
Flower center: pink 3" tight circle
Peg for back: turquoise 2" tight circle
Glue the petals together, and then add the flower center.
Glue the peg to the back of the flower.

Small Flowers (make two)

Petals: six turquoise 3" marquises
Flower center: pink 2" tight circle
Glue the petals together, and then add the flower center.

Leaves and Scrolls
Scrolls: two teal 3" loose scrolls
Leaves: two teal 3" marquises
Glue the leaves to the scrolls.

• Assembly
Using the photo as a guide, glue the butterfly onto the background.

Then position and glue the large flower.

Add the two small flowers and the two scrolls with leaves.

Pattern for Circus Clown on page 132. Enlarge by 140%.

Circus Clown

Perfect for a child's bedroom, this strikingly colorful and happy figure will look best in a frame. Highlight one of its brightest colors with a matching mat.

Use 1/8"-wide paper unless another width is specified. See pattern on page 131.

Head and Face
First, glue five 24" lengths of flesh paper together, end to end.

Then, using this 120" length, roll a rounded grape roll to serve as the clown's head.

Create the curly hair by layering orange 3" loose circles.

With acrylics, paint in the eyes, nose, and mouth. (Cut and glue these pieces if you'd rather; make the eyes with small dots cut from black paper and the nose and mouth from a triangle and a crescent cut from red paper.)

Hat
Make the brim by rolling a black 18" narrow crescent.

Fill in the outline of the crown with black 3" marquises and teardrops.

Glue the crown to the brim, and add a length of narrow red paper as a hat band.

Add a turquoise 4" fringed flower to the hat band.

Shirt and Pants
Fill in both outlines on this page with bright yellow 3" marquises and triangles.

Glue the pants and shirt together, placing the shirt so that it overlaps the pants slightly.

The neck ruffle is made in two sections. Make one section with three bright yellow 5" bunny ears and the other section with two bunny ears. Set the sections aside.

Make each sleeve ruffle with three bright yellow 4" bunny ears.

Make each ruffle for the pants with four bright yellow 5" bunny ears.

Glue a length of turquoise along the edge of each ruffle.

Glue each ruffle to the suit at an angle.

Make three turquoise 4" fringed flowers, and add these as buttons.

Using a round hole punch, make fourteen polka dots in a variety of colors, and glue them to the shirt and pants.

Mittens and Shoes
Fill in the mitten outlines with turquoise 3" marquises and teardrops.

Roll a black 4" rectangle for the heel of each shoe.

Fill in the rest of the shoe outline with black 3" marquises and crescents.

Balloons (make eight)
First roll a 24" length of any brightly colored paper, and let it expand in the largest mold on the designer board. Then shape an eccentric teardrop from it.

Add a 3" bunny ear (in the same color) to the teardrop's point.

Make a balloon string by gluing a narrow strip of black paper to the bunny ear.

• Assembly
Glue the hat to the head and the head to the collar.

Glue the mittens to the sleeves so that the sleeves overlap them slightly.

Glue the shoes to the pants.

Position the balloons; then glue them in place.

Gather the balloon strings, trim them to the proper length, and glue their ends to the upraised mitten's back.

See pattern on page 131.

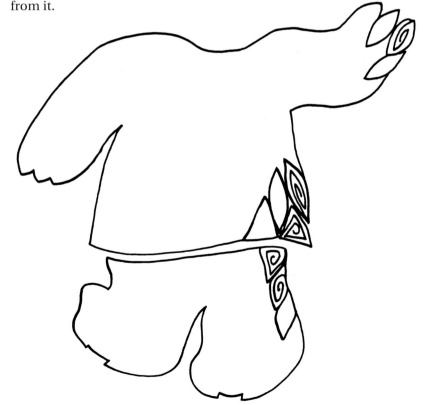

A Gallery

If you've ever doubted that quilling designs can be as different from one another as the artists who create them, browse through the next few pages. In them, you'll find some examples of today's best quillwork. Let these pieces and their makers inspire you as you move toward originating your own designs.

The quillwork featured here was generated by people who, like you, were once beginners.

With patience, practice, imagination, and skill, these designers learned to translate the humble techniques of quilling into wonderfully personal and artistically distinct forms. Some of their works are playful, others are steeped in tradition, and still others are studies in color and design. Yet they all share two things: the exceptional skill with which they were made and their creators' love for their craft.

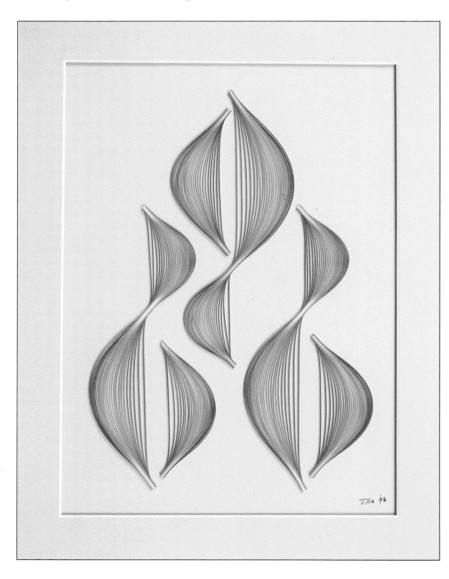

Abstracts

Some of today's finest quilling designs forego rolled shapes in favor of simple but elegant arrangements of shaped lengths of paper. Trees Tra, the Dutch designer of these abstracts, makes optimum use of clean lines, color, and balance to transform quilling strips into impressive visual studies.

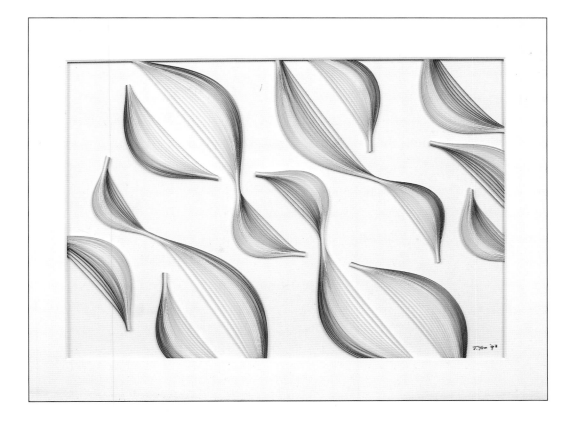

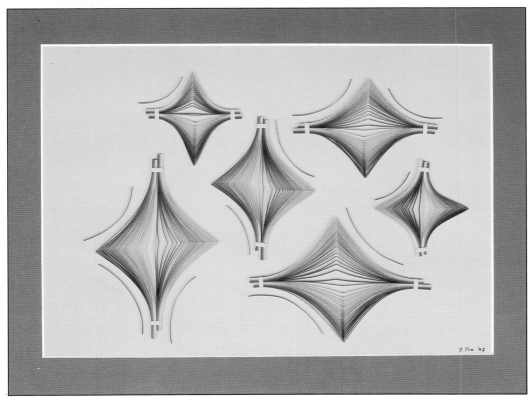

Carpet Page

This stunning design, by Naomi Lipsky, was inspired by an Islamic window carving. Its color scheme is derived from a Persian carpet. The coils of the vase and some of the leaves are gilt-edged with 23-karat gold leaf, and the bevel of the mat is also gilt.

Two Quilled Boxes

*These two boxes are embellished with elaborate quillwork.
English designer Brenda Rhodes has carefully selected colors to complement the containers and has made excellent
use of the English technique known as huskings.*

Japanese Garden

Set into a glass-topped table, this three-dimensional arrangement illustrates one of the many captivating forms that quillwork can take. By combining the graceful symmetry of snow-white, quilled spider mums and quilled cherry blossoms with the asymmetry of weathered wood, designer Joyce Bennett has created a perfect—and distinctly oriental—balance between opposites.

Shell Necklace and Earrings

Naomi Lipsky has blended creativity, skill, and patience to design and quill this magnificent necklace and earring set, which won First Prize and Best of Show for crafts at the Maryland State Fair and First Prize at the Minnesota State Fair. The paper is 1/8"-wide, acid-free, and hand-cut. Some of the coils have been hand-gilt with 23-karat gold leaf; the findings are also gold.

The Three Festivals

Naomi Lipsky's quilled designs represent the three Pilgrim festivals of the Biblical calendar, each of which has agricultural as well as historical significance. From left to right, the scenes depict Passover, which began with Moses in the bulrushes, Shevuoth, which celebrates the giving of the Ten Commandments at Mt. Sinai, and Sukkoth, the festival of the harvest.

Chess Pieces

These three-dimensional, quilled pieces by Naomi Lipsky are part of an entire set, which was featured in the first juried exhibit of contemporary gilding, at the Newark Museum in New Jersey. Each piece is made entirely from tight coils of standard width quilling paper, is approximately 3" high and 1" in diameter, and is topped with shaped vertical coils, hand-gilt on both sides with 23-karat gold leaf. The set was varnished with acrylic matte medium.

Gingerbread House

This playful structure took imaginative designer Patricia Caputo twenty-six hours to make. The base, formed with reinforced poster board, is completely covered with quilled shapes. Its gingerbread walls and the icing-like roof and trim colors make this three-dimensional piece seem almost edible.

Willow Pattern Plate

This intricately quilled design, which won the Quilling Guild's highest award in 1989, took designer Margaret Haigh six months' of evening work to complete. Quilled in four shades of blue, the traditional china pattern conveys both depth and motion.

Acknowledgements

Many thanks to

Florian Papp Gallery (New York) for permission to reproduce the photographs by Richard Goodbody on pages 8, 10, and 12. The captions that accompany these are derived from the Florian Papp publication *Rolled, Scrolled, Crimped and Folded: The Lost Art of Filigree Paperwork.*

The New Berlin Co., Inc., Muskego, WI, for the loan of their Country Keepers (page 59).

Ken Brown's Studio of Calligraphic Art in Hugo, Oklahoma, for permission to reproduce Ken's calligraphy (page 105), and verse and calligraphy (page 115).

The following publications, for permission to reprint the author's published designs:

Craftworks for the Home, May 1993. All American Crafts, Inc., Newark, NJ (Kitchen Herbs, page 36)

Crafts Country Christmas, Crafts Magazine. PJS Publications, Inc., Peoria, IL (Christmas Sampler, © 1987, page 60)

Crafting Today, Oct. 1990. All American Crafts, Inc., Newton, NJ (Fridge Magnets, page 97)

My sincere thanks to the contributing designers; I am fortunate to have such talented friends share their designs.

Contributing Designers

Virginia Alexander (Free-Standing Quilled Figures, pages 117-119) is a self-taught quiller who has won an award at the International Festival of Quilling, where she demonstrated the techniques that she uses to make her three-dimensional *Jinisans*. Virginia lives in Rochester, New York.

Eleanor Baxter (Valentine Hang-Up, pages 79-80; Floral Gift Tags, pages 92-93) describes quilling as her first love. For ten years, she was the office manager of Lake City Craft Company; she now creates quilling designs and has generously provided the author of this book with both ideas and advice. Eleanor resides in Kansas City, Missouri.

Joyce Bennett (Japanese Garden, page 138), who lives in Corona, California, is a free-lance consultant, craft designer, and author of many books. She has been an editor at several crafts magazines and has worked extensively with silk and dried flowers, as well as with quilling. Joyce is host of a PBS television series entitled *Naturally Floral.*

Patricia Caputo (Calla Lily Border Design, pages 88-89; Chess Board, pages 105-106; Gingerbread House, page 140) serves as a representative to the Quilling Guild of England and writes a newsletter, *Quill America*, for its American members. She resides in Enfield, Connecticut, where she teaches quilling and runs her business, Whimsiquills. Pat sells her work through shops in both New York and Florida.

Jan Cole, of Palm Beach Garden, Florida, is an expert quiller whose commissions come from as far away as Hungary and Japan. She specializes in quilling for weddings, anniversaries, and bar mitzvahs and has designed a convenient hanger for quilling strips (page 20).

Margaret Haigh's Willow Pattern Plate (page 141) won the Quilling Guild Salvar, the highest award given at the Guild's annual general meeting, in 1989. She serves as the Guild's archivist and is also a regional representative. Margaret lives in Melksham, Wiltshire (England).

Naomi Geller Lipsky (Bird Shalom, pages 42-43; Bridal Canopy Border Design, pages 90-92; Carpet Page, page 136; Shell Necklace and Earrings and The Three Festivals, page 139; Chess Pieces, page 140), a resident of Rochester, Minnesota, retired from a career in biochemistry to become a free-lance decorative artist. She serves on the Board of Directors of the Southeast Minnesota Visual Artists and is the Coordinator of the SEMVA Art Gallery and Education Center. Though the majority of Naomi's quillwork is privately commissioned, some pieces have been displayed in juried shows.

Yvonne McGarry (Quilling on Lace Eggs, pages 82-83), who lives in Omaha, Nebraska, learned to quill when she became involved with a fund-raising project—making and selling quilled eggs—started by her local chapter of the Pilot Club. Her husband, Fred, after watching Yvonne use scissors to cut fringes, designed the fringers described in this book.

Eileen Maddox (Quilt-Block Ornaments, page 64), who is an expert quilter and quilt designer, adapts her favorite quilt-block designs for use in quilling. She enjoys graphic designing with a computer as well. Eileen lives in Grandview, Missouri, and participates in eight craft fairs each year.

Jody Ondrus (Quilled Wreath, pages 46-47; Quillwork for Coasters, pages 99-101; Quilled Flower Hat, pages 110-111), whose specialty is quilled floral designs, also works with silk and dried flowers. She is an American representative of the Quilling Guild of England, the founder of the Quilling Club of Northwest Ohio, and a member of the Society of Craft Designers. Her patterns have been published in several craft magazines. Jody lives in Maple Heights, Ohio, and her business is named *Blossoms 'n Bows.*

Brenda Rhodes (Quilled Boxes, page 137), for whom quilling is a "ruling passion," taught herself